Andrea and Tobias Kostial

Lofoten
and Vesterålen

60 walks in the land of the midnight sun

ROTHER

PREFACE

The Lofoten are a group of islands of remarkable Nordic beauty – with rock formations billions of years old, glacially formed mountain ranges, bogs and lakes, white sandy beaches, deep fjords and rocks that stand with their pointed and smooth-sided peaks like a wall in the Norwegian Sea. A paradise for walkers who, within a few hundred vertical metres, can venture into alpine territory and be rewarded with fantastic views. The less tourist-developed and more unknown Vesterålen are also a walking area par excellence. The walker can expect a diversity of landscapes from the highest peak of the archipelago to alpine regions of only 400m above sea level and the large Andøya bogs.

Whether fishing villages or prehistoric lakes, cave paintings, Vikings or Lofoten fishermen, stone age tombs or 'Skulpturlandskap' (sculptures in the landscape), drying racks for fish or cod liver oil factories – there's plenty to explore inbetween all the steeply ascending tracks and old fishermen's paths. In the museums you can learn a lot about life in earlier times when the village kings were in charge and the fish farmers had to work hard to make a living. And in the small cemeteries the lonely resting places of the women testify to the wet grave of their husbands – the Norwegian Sea.

The most spectacular and beautiful time to visit the Lofoten and Vesterålen is during the midnight sun in the summer. For when night becomes day, the sun bathes the islands in a memorable light. The opportunity to go walking at this 'time of day', to stand on a summit or look into the distance across the Norwegian Sea, is a special experience. But other times of the year also have their charm with, for example, the polar lights, the darkness or Lofoten fishing.

With our guide book we hope to introduce you to the Lofoten and Vesterålen, a mountain world which we have hiked together. There is a path onto almost every peak of the archipelago, sometimes only faintly visible, at other times well used. Our choice of walks ranges from easier walks you can do with the family to challenging walks. Each walk includes information and tips about places worth seeing along the way.

We would like you to treat this corner of the earth with care, to respect the people of the Lofoten and Vesterålen, to make use of the offers made available in the form of campsites and permanent accommodation and thus be able to take many positive memories back home with you.

Spring 2025

Andrea and Tobias Kostial
lofoten-reisen.de

View down to Henningsvær.

CONTENTS

Preface...3
Overview map...6
Top walks...8
General information..11
    Grades..12
    GPS tracks and coordinates of the starting points.....13
    Symbols..15
    Allemannsretten – the right to roam........................16
    Lofoten Code of Conduct...17
Useful tips..26
    Emergency numbers..29
    Leisure time and sport...30
    Short walking glossary..35

Walking on the Lofoten.......................................38

#	Time	Walk	Page
1	3.30 hrs	Røstlandet	44
2	5.45 hrs	Måstad and Måstadheia, 407m	50
3	2.00 hrs	Håen, 438m	54
TOP 4	4.30 hrs	Munkebu, 405m	56
5	8.00 hrs	Hermannsdalstinden, 1029m	60
6	2.20 hrs	Vindstad – Bunesstranda	64
TOP 7	3.10 hrs	Reinebringen, 484m	66
8	2.00 hrs	Solbjørnvatnet and Tekoppstetten, 365m	69
TOP 9	3.00 hrs	Kvalvika	72
10	4.20 hrs	Ryten, 543m	76
11	1.20 hrs	Mulstøa	78
12	2.00 hrs	Litlberget, 281m	80
13	2.30 hrs	Volandstinden, 457m	82
14	2.30 hrs	Flakstadtinden, 484m	84
TOP 15	4.00 hrs	From Nesland to Nusfjord	86
16	4.30 hrs	Tønsåsheia, 769m	90
17	2.00 hrs	Napp – Andopen	92
18	3.30 hrs	Stornappstinden, 740m	94
19	3.30 hrs	Skottinden, 671m	96
20	2.30 hrs	Ballstadheia with Nonstinden, 459m	98
21	1.30 hrs	Hornsheia, 153m	100
22	2.30 hrs	Offersøykammen, 436m	102
23	2.15 hrs	On old paths between Haukland and Utakleiv	104
24	4.30 hrs	Himmeltindan, 931m	106
25	2.30 hrs	Along the coastal path between Eggum and Unstad	109
26	4.15 hrs	Steinetinden, 509m	112
27	5.00 hrs	Justadtinden, 738m	115
28	2.15 hrs	Brattflogan, 460m	118

29	2.00 hrs	Vetten, 414m	122
30	3.45 hrs	Haveren, 808m	124
TOP 31	1.45 hrs	Hoven, 368m	128
32	3.00 hrs	Festvågtinden, 541m	131
33	2.15 hrs	Glomtinden, 419m	134
34	2.30 hrs	Tjeldbergtinden, 367m	136
35	2.15 hrs	Tuva, 477m	138
36	3.00 hrs	Fløya, 590m	141
37	3.00 hrs	Walking on the island of Skrova	144
38	4.00 hrs	Suolovarri (Rundfjellet), 803m	147
TOP 39	4.30 hrs	Matmora, 788m	150
40	5.00 hrs	Geitgallien, 1085m	154
TOP 41	1.45 hrs	Keiservarden, 384m	156
42	2.30 hrs	The Dronningstien on Årsteinen (Stortinden), 530m	160

Walking on the Vesterålen 162

43	3.00 hrs	Trollfjordhytta, 405m	168
44	5.30 hrs	Strøna, 906m	172
45	5.30 hrs	Lamlitinden, 657m	174
46	2.00 hrs	Finnsæterkollen, 439m	177
TOP 47	10.30 hrs	Møysalen, 1262m	180
48	3 days	Multi-day walk through the Møysalen nasjonalpark	184
49	7.30 hrs	Snytindhytta, 390m	192
50	4.30 hrs	Stortinden, 1021m	195
51	4.30 hrs	Skata, 736m	198
52	2.30 hrs	Veten, 467m	201
53	3.00 hrs	Breitinden, 598m	204
54	1.30 hrs	Vikan	206
55	0.45 hrs	Bufjellet, 210m	210
56	2.50 hrs	Trollan, 543m	212
57	3.15 hrs	Nonskollen, 611m	214
TOP 58	5.30 hrs	Dronningruta – the queen's route	216
TOP 59	2.45 hrs	Coastal paths between Stave and Bleik	220
60	2.00 hrs	Røyken, 468m	226

Index 228

TOP WALKS

Munkebu
This varied walk leads into the centre of Moskenesøya island. You ascend past waterfalls and along prehistoric lakes over alpine terrain up to 400m. From here you also have a good starting point for the ascent of Hermannsdalstinden, 1029m *(Walk 4, 4.30 hrs)*.

Kvalvika
This circular walk to the other side of Moskenesøya takes you along small lakes and rock massifs that are billions of years old to two sandy beaches *(Walk 9, 3.00 hrs)*.

Nesland – Nusfjord
This varied walk for walkers and their children runs along an old coastal path that connects the small fishing villages of Nesland and Nusfjord with each other *(Walk 15, 4.00 hrs)*.

Reinebringen
The most popular walk on the entire archipelago. It offers magnificent panoramic views, but can get very busy. *(Walk 7, 3.10 hrs)*.

Hoven
Hoven rises up out of its boggy surroundings on Gimsøya like a shark's fin. And inspite of its low altitude it gives you the feeling of being up really high *(Walk 31, 1.45 hrs)*.

Matmora
An enchanting light birchwood, alpine terrain and a summit panorama along the north side of the Lofoten as far as the western foothills of Vesterålen *(Walk 39, 4.30 hrs)*.

Dronningruta
The Dronningruta from Nyksund to Stø and back runs along the coastline and then circles back across the mountain range above *(Walk 58, 5.30 hrs)*.

Keiservarden
Kaiser Wilhelm II once erected a cairn on the top of Digermulkollen. From here you are afforded views across the Raftsundet and along the Lofoten chain *(Walk 41, 1.45 hrs)*.

Måtinden
A short ascent, a walk across an extensive high plateau and at your destination a gigantic 'cliff': brilliant sandy beaches far below you with the endless Norwegian Sea stretching out ahead *(Walk 59, 2.45 hrs)*.

Møysalen
The highest and most striking mountain of Vesterålen, 1262m, lies in the national park of the same name and this long walk brings you into a delightful region of Norway *(Walk 47, 10.30 hrs)*.

Taking care of the environment ...

When we are out hiking, we also leave an ecological footprint, however, being in harmony with the environment is not that difficult!

PREPARATION AND GETTING THERE
- Before you go, find out what you can do to protect the nature and the environment in the hiking area you are visiting.
- Wherever possible, use public transport such as busses and trains as well as hiking busses.
- If you travel by car, share the ride with others.
- If it's a long drive to the starting point, plan multi-day trips or find a local guesthouse from where you can do several walks.
- Try to limit air travel as much as possible and offset it by contributing to climate protection projects.

CLOTHING AND EQUIPMENT
- Buy environmentally friendly and fair-trade outdoor gear and use your clothes as long as possible.
- You can also buy second hand equipment or use rental gear.
- Fix broken things rather than buying new equipment.

FOOD
- Make sure you buy organic food as well as regional and seasonal products.
- Stay in huts and guesthouses that offer local products.
- Bring your own water bottle and sandwich box instead of buying disposable bottles or food that is wrapped in plastic.

ACCOMMODATION
- Book your accommodation directly with the locals, so they can benefit.
- Save electricity and water in huts and other places you stay in.

WHEN WALKING
- Use designated trails and avoid shortcuts.
- Respect closed trails and conservation areas.
- Don't pick flowers or take plants home with you.
- Respect forest fire warnings.
- Take your rubbish with you and dispose of it at home.
- If possible, avoid going to the toilet in the open.
- Avoid noise.
- Put your dog on a leash.

GENERAL INFORMATION

Use of the guide book
The guide book contains 42 suggested walks on the Lofoten and 18 on the Vesterålen. In so doing, the administrative assignment of the islands to the respective archipelago was taken into account. And so although Keiservarden actually lies on the island of Hinnøya which belongs to Vesterålen, it is administratively located in the Vågan municipality (Lofoten). Trollfjordhytta and Strøna, on the other hand, belong to the Vesterålen inspite of their location on the island of Austvågøya. General maps on the back cover and on pages 6/7 provide an overview of the location of each individual walk.

Grade
Apart from a few exceptions most of the walks described in this guide are unmarked natural paths which are usually well-trodden and lead across areas of meadow or heathland, rock, areas or scree. The building or maintenance of paths is rare. This results in the use of your hands or the circumnavigation of a boggy area is more frequently necessary than you are used to in other regions of Europe. Most summit ascents will involve short sections of steep inclines. The ascent of vertical metres by means of zigzag paths is virtually non-existent. The transistion into the vegetation-free zone occurs from a height of 300 to 400m. This means that the terrain becomes more stony and rocky from this altitude upwards. The alpine and high alpine terrain begins from an altitude of about 600m. Extremely exposed sections in places require a higher degree of concentration.

The Trollfjordhytta.

Snow may persist into early summer at altitudes of 400m upwards and here you might come across snowfields and large amounts of boggy terrain caused by the melting snow. Sheep tracks might lead you the wrong way sometimes so be careful to pay extra attention in these places. You are advised not to undertake any of the walks in thick cloud, fog and heavy rainfall because the risks in terms of route finding and your safety are too large. In order to be aware of impending changes in the weather you should regularly check the very good forecast from the Norwegian Metereological Institute (yr.no) which gives detailed weather information for towns and sometimes even summits.

The individual walks are graded blue, red or black and this gives you an immediate indication of the level of difficulty.

GRADES

■ = Easy
These walks frequently involve gentle ascents, they are not exposed and require no particular skills. They are suitable for beginners and children.

■ = Moderate
These walks are mostly characterised by steep ascents and descents. They overcome longer distances and require the use of your hands in some places. Surefootedness and a good head for heights are often necessary.

■ = Difficult
Difficult walks require a much higher demand on fitness and stamina. The walks run mostly at altitudes of over 900m, in places over rough alpine terrain with no paths; a good head for heights, surefootedness as well as experience in walking in the mountains are vital.

Walking times
The walking times in this guide refer to the actual times of a walker of average fitness, i.e. about 4km an hour over level ground and about 400 vertical metres an hour on ascent. Weather, terrain, personal physical shape, consideration of fellow hikers and many other factors determine the actual walking time.

Maps
For the Lofoten there are available the following waterproof maps published by Nordeca (turkart) to a scale of 1:50,000: Vest-Lofoten, Vestvågøy and also Vågan. For Vesterålen there are the maps Vesterålen – Hinnøya Sør and also Vesterålen – Hinnøya Nord to a scale of 1:100,000. These form the basis of the maps in this guide. In its Høyfjellskart series, the Swedish map publisher Calazo has produced the following waterproof maps

GPS TRACKS AND COORDINATES OF THE STARTING POINTS

On **gps.rother.de**, GPS tracks and coordinates of the starting points are available for free download which can be accessed by scanning this QR code.
3rd edition, password: 484103meg
The GPS tracks can be imported into the **Rother App**. The app tells you exactly where you are and where you are going when you are on the move. You can find instructions on **rother.de/gps**
As possible changes and errors can never be ruled out completely, we advise you to never entirely rely on GPS data for orientation, but to assess the conditions on the ground.

to a scale of 1:30,000: Moskenesøya & Flakstadøya, Austvågøya & Svolvær as well as Vestvågøya, Leknes. The Norwegian Mapping Authority Statens Kartverk provides official maps of Norway as well as aerial photographs on its website at norgeskart.no. The site allows you to print individual sections of a map. The Norgeskart Outdoors app also provides outstanding service.

High above Kvalvika.

Equipment
All types of weather conditions must be taken into account on the archipelagos, even during the warmer months of the year. Temperatures under 10 °C and strong winds can be experienced even in high summer, but if the temperatures rise above 18 °C you can look forward to a refreshing dip in the sea. So, together with sturdy, waterproof (!!) footwear and possibly gaiters, the appropriate clothing for every weather condition is essential, including swimwear.

Waymarking and signposts
The waymarkers and signposts with which you are familiar in southern Norway walking regions and the Alps, only exist in very few cases on the Lofoten. You should be careful with the walking maps (turkart). The routes coloured red in these maps do not denote waymarked routes. The Vesterålen Turlag (trekking association) has been trying for years to introduce signposts on the more frequently used walking paths in Vesterålen, as well as uniform waymarkers throughout.

Walking with children
We have walked almost every one of the walks described in this book with one or several of our children. Everyone should be responsible for making the decision as to which walks are suitable for their own children depending on their age and fitness. We have marked some of the walks with the symbol 'suitable for children'. These walks have particular qualities: they are either

especially short and easy walks, or they offer a day's walk with a variety of interest along the way. On some more challenging walks we make special reference to attractive and interesting sections which are suitable for less experienced walkers.

Trekking and mountain sports association, mountain huts/cabins

The Lofoten Turlag (LT) and the Vesterålen Turlag (VT) are member associations of the Norwegian Trekking Association DNT (Den Norske Turistforening). The LT operates 3 closed mountain cabins (Munkebu on Moskenesøya, Selfjord on the Fjord of the same name on Moskenesøya in the municipality of Flakstadøya and also the Nøkksætra at Svolvær). The key is only available to members of the DNT.

The VT operates several mountain cabins (including Guvåghytta, Ingemannhytta, Snytindhytta and Trollfjordhytta). The cabins are open all year round, but some of them require a key to get in. You can book beds at the huts at ut.no and vesteralen.dnt.no. All cabins are comfortably equipped self-catering cabins but without provisions.

There are no reciprocal rights for other walking associations except for the Scandinavian ones.

You can find more information at lofoten.dnt.no and vesteralen.dnt.no.

SYMBOLS

Symbols in the tour headings
- accessible by bus/train
- reachable by ferry
- refreshment
- suitable for children

Symbols for height profiles
- village with bar/restaurant
- restaurant, café, dairy
- self-catering mountain hut, cabin, rorbuer, hostel
- refuge, shelter, gapahuk

- campsite
- car park
- ferry dock
- skilift
- summit, peak
- pass, col
- lighthouse, navigational light
- cave
- viewpoint
- church, chapel, monastery
- sandy beach, public beach

Friluftsliv and allemannsretten

The life of a Norwegian is unthinkable without friluftsliv: being active in the open countryside, walking, fishing, hunting, skiing or any other non-motorised form of activity, belongs to the Norwegian way of thinking. This frequently occurs in a really unconventional way: swimming in 12 degree temperatures in the Norwegian Sea, summiting a peak 300 times in a year or overtaking the fully equipped Continental European in gym shoes with a coolbag under his arm and a baby on his back – nothing seems impossible for a Norwegian. Therefore be careful when local people make suggestions for allegedly quick and especially easy walks – they are tough people here, no marsh is too wet, no path is too unclear, no rock face is too steep!

The basis of this love of all activities in natural surroundings is the allemannsretten (the right to roam). As a fundamental requirement it expects the respectful handling of nature and the consideration for farmers, landowners and other visitors. The right of access applies to **non-motorised** activities. Wild camping with mobile homes in every conceivable location is not desirable. Rising numbers of tourists (both tourists from abroad and Norway) and the associated, ever increasing misuse of the law has already led to consider restrictions in the future. Therefore all travellers, whether walking or driving, should observe the basic rules (see box Allemannsretten).

ALLEMANNSRETTEN – THE RIGHT TO ROAM

- Anyone on foot or skies is allowed to roam freely and take a rest on open, 'unfenced' or unbuilt land.
- 'Fenced' land (this does not necessarily mean with actual fences) is private land and includes farmed land, fields, pastures, gardens, orchards, building sites and industrial areas.
- Apart from cultivated fields and car parks you are allowed to put up a tent at a distance of at least 150m from a building or sleep under the open sky. If you do this for longer than 2 days you need to ask permission from the landowner.
- The emptying of camp toilets can only be done in designated places.
- Open fires are forbidden in and around wooded areas from the 15th April to the 15th September.
- In general the picking of berries, mushrooms and flowers is allowed. Cloudberries may only be eaten on the spot and not collected.

Walking inside the national park

The Lofotodden nasjonalpark (Walks 6, 7, 10–13) became the 45th Norwegian national park when it was established in 2018. The walks on Vesterålen lead through the Møysalen nasjonalpark (Walks 47 and 48).

On the walks within the park borders, the allemannsretten rules largely apply. However, every park has different rules that must be observed. This includes general overnight stays, flying drones and the use of non-motorised bikes (e-bikes are not allowed).

The respective rules can be found on information boards and in information leaflets.

LOFOTEN CODE OF CONDUCT

- Camp in designated areas.
- Leave no trace.
- Follow the path and avoid the creation of new paths.
- Throw waste in the waste bins.
- Use public toilets.
- Respect private property.
- Be considerate in traffic.
- Ban on fires.
- Respect wildlife.

The complete Code of Conduct can be found at lofoten.info/lofotencodeofconduct.

Tourism on the Lofoten

Over the last few years the Lofoten have become one of the most popular travel destinations in Norway. The number of native as well as foreign visitors is increasing and confronts the inhabitants of the archipelago with new difficulties: higher traffic numbers, the overuse of favourite locations as well as overnight stops by motorhome owners and campers in car parks and private property along the roads, and even in cemeteries. Wild camping with cars, tents and camper vans in every conceivable spot is not

On Snøtindan with the striking peak of Møysalen in the background.

only inconsiderate, but goes against the guidelines of the allemannsretten. The freedom to roam refers specifically to any **non-motorised** type of movement and staying overnight in places away from urban areas, in the so-called utmark. The Lofoten are the most densely populated area in northern Norway and you should be well aware that practically every piece of land where you might want to put up your tent is on private property. Respecting the do's and don'ts, as well as discreet interaction with the places where you decide to stay for a while, should be the first and last thing every traveller thinks about.

Lofoten Friluftsrad has developed a map indicating infrastructure, including public toilets, camper van recycling sites, natural reserves, and areas where camping is not permitted... lofotenfriluft.no/turistkart.

Best walking season

The best walking season on the archipelagos are the months between the middle of June and the end of September. The temperatures are at their highest until the middle of August, the big snow melt in the mountains has passed and the 'eternal' light makes walking into a unique experience. At the latest from the middle of August onwards it is noticeably darker, cooler and very desolate although now is the chance for seeing the northern lights. The mørketid (polar night) rapidly approaches from the end of September.

Descent from Ryten.

On the way to the Litlberget.

The best walking season also coincides with the Norwegian school holidays. Holiday time here means both vacation time and high season. The Lofoten are, at the moment, the most popular internal domestic destination for Norwegians. This means that places of accommodation and museums are often full, particularly in July. However, museums have extended opening hours in the holiday period and the ferries operate a summer schedule.

Multi-day walks

Neither the Lofoten nor the Vesterålen are typical long distance walking regions. One exception is the walking area of Møysalen on the island of Hinnøya (Walk 48). The mountain cabins operated by the Lofoten Turlag and the Vesterålen Turlag are mostly starting points for walks and ski tours in the areas where the cabins are located. Nevertheless, it is possible to combine various sections of different routes or extend them into a multi-day walk. However, you need to be particularly careful on these walks when choosing where to sleep. Do not camp too close to water or mires, do not use soap or anything similar, and remember to take all rubbish away with you, including toilet paper, and do not bury or burn anything. The tents used for such expeditions should be made of material with the highest possible wind resistance and a three-season sleeping bag is recommended. There usually aren't any problems with sources of water, but be careful in areas where there are sheep grazing. Otherwise be sure to follow the code of the right to roam.

Descent from Matmora, 788m.

Climate, weather

The warm water of the North Atlantic Drift which runs along the Norwegian coastline bestows upon the Lofoten and Vesterålen islands (they lie at the same latitude as Baffin Island, Northern Siberia and Greenland) a temperate maritime climate. This becomes evident with the relatively cool summers and warm winters. The islands of Røst and Værøy are the most northern islands in the world with average annual temperatures above freezing point (the largest positive temperature anomaly relative to its latitude).

July and August, statistically with an average temperature of 12 °C, are seen as the warmest months. Nevertheless temperatures of 20 °C and above are not unheard of. The temperatures generally feel warmer on the islands and it's not uncommon to walk in shorts and a T-Shirt. Even with temperatures of 18 °C many feel the desire to take a cooling swim.

A particular weather phenomenon takes place on days with nice weather. Sea mist forms above the Norwegian Sea which northwesterly winds force against the Lofoten wall. While fog persists on the outside, the coast on the Vestfjorden enjoys nothing but sunshine. A similar thing happens with northwest winds and rain clouds: while it's raining over the Norwegian Sea, the sun is shining only a few kilometres away on Vestfjorden.

The average temperature of the coldest months January and February is −1 °C, but the temperatures can also fall to −10 °C. The areas around the coast frequently remain snow and ice-free. In the higher regions, however, snow can be expected during the whole of winter and ski tours are some of the popular leisure time activities.

Precipitation lies on average between 1000 and 1500mm and the months of May and June are the driest months. In the autumn and winter the winds become noticeably stronger with average speeds of 18/19 miles per hour. Prolonged periods with winds of 35/45 miles per hour are not uncommon. Since the local weather can differ significantly at a distance of a few kilometres because of the topography of the islands, it's always worth taking a look at the weather forecast.

The website of the Norwegian Meteorological Institute (yr.no) provides detailed weather forecasts for every location. You can download their mobile app from their website. The storm.no website is another good source for weather forecasts.

Winter climb onto Fløya.

Polar lights on the Vaterfjordpollen.

Midnight sun and polar night

The phenomenon north of the polar circle, determined by the tilting of the earth's axis, is called the midnight sun when the sun does not set for a longish period of time, the length of which depends on the latitude. Conversely, in winter, it comes round to the so-called mørketid – polar night. When night becomes day the biorhythm of nature changes. Plants, animals and humans have shortened rest periods, fill up with energy and work this off. People, young and old, are on the move at times where they usually sleep. In their private lives they potter around and party until deep into the 'night'. Not until soon after midnight does nature come to rest.

The sun reaches its lowest point at around 1am in the north, then, after a short pause, rises again. On fine days you have the most intensive gradations of light at this time. If you are staying in the far north be sure not to miss this amazing sight. The best places to see the lights are located on the north side of the archipelagos where you have an open view across the Norwegian Sea.

During the time of the polar night the sun barely rises above the horizon. However, there is still a noticeable difference between night and day. During the day a kind of twilight illuminates the polar night.

	midnight sun	**polar night**
Svolvær	24 May – 17 July	4 December – 8 January
Andenes	19 May – 23 July	27 November – 15 January

Aurora borealis

Polar lights occur in the upper atmospheric zone of the upper atmosphere (100–200km) when small charged electromagnetic particles from the sun meet atoms of oxygen and nitrogen and stimulate those atoms, causing them to light up. The frequency and intensity depend on the solar activity cycle. The Lofoten and Vesterålen are located under the aurora oval (an area forming a ring around the magnetic pole) and are therefore an advantageous place from which to observe the lights which occur from the end of August when the nights become dark again, to the beginning of April. The polar lights appear as diffuse surfaces, bands, arcs, rays, coronas in varying degrees of intensity – mostly green in colour. Sometimes they make only a short appearance then again they astonish you for hours on end. A truly fantastic spectacle, only if the sky is clear, of course.

Geology

The basis of the Lofoten and Vesterålen consists of rocks from the time of the first formation of the mainland in the Precambrian. The Langøya and Hinnøya (Vesterålen) islands are characterised by orthogneiss and small greenstone belts. The age of these rocks is over 2.5 billion years. The paragneiss of the Lofoten dates from the Palaeoproterozoic (1.6–2.5 billion years ago). Over 50 percent of the Lofoten consist of different types of plutonites (igneous plutonic rocks) and are considerably younger (about 1.8 billion years old). The rocks passed through several uplifts, subsidence and folds; the last crucial exposure of these ancient layers took place around 10 million years ago.

During the last ice age around 10,000 years ago, the Lofoten didn't lie under the up to three kilometre thick ice sheet of Scandinavia, but passed through several phases of local glaciations. There existed cirque glaciers and, simultaneously, mountain peaks rising up out of the ice (Nunataks)

Midnight sun above Litløya and Gaukværøya.

which were exposed to the forces of weathering. In this way the unique landscape was created with its peaks and steep mountain rock faces. The glacial characteristics can be seen most noticeably on the islands of Moskenesøya and Austvågøya.

The biggest cold water coral reef in Norway with over 100km² was discovered to the west of the island of Røst in 2002 at the edge of the continental shelf, and was put under a protection order in 2003.

Since large quantities of oil and gas were suspected to be located offshore, the activities of the oil and gas industry have been increased. A widespread alliance of local residents, environmentalists and fishermen (folkeaksjonen.no) successfully fought against the exploration of these natural resources which would have threatened the island life of the Lofoten and Vesterålen, as well as the island of Senja. Their struggle resulted in these plans being abandoned.

Flora and fauna

At first glance both archipelagos appear to be covered in very bare vegetation. Wide stretches of the Lofoten are treeless which, on the one hand is due to the topographical conditions, and on the other hand is thanks to the deforestation in earlier times. There are areas of forest on Vesterålen especially in regions further away from the coast. The birch tree is the most frequent tree to be seen on both archipelagos. Stands of fir trees have their origin in reforestation measures apart from a few exceptions. Salt-resistant beach plants or types of saxifrage dominate the coastal stretches given the right conditions. But only a short way from the shoreline begin the cultivated, intensively used agricultural areas (green stuff; potatoes and strawberries are also grown in more sheltered areas on Vesterålen). Here you will find the rosebay willowherb ever-present in Scandinavia.

Large areas, however, are covered by extensive bogs together with their typical vegetation such as cotton grass, sundew and cloudberries (Gimsøya, Andøya). But also in the mountainous regions there are boggy areas eve-

Orca family with young. *Oystercatchers.*

Beautiful flowers in spring: moss campion and wild pansies.

rywhere, in valleys and on gentle slopes, which are interspersed with ferns and light forests of small growing birch with up to 100 year old specimens. In drier areas you will find junipers and pastures. The birch forest recedes with increasing altitude, the tree line starts at 150 metres above sea level and the moorlands of dwarf shrubs follow on. Dense cushions of blueberries, Swedish dwarf cornel, cranberries, crowberries and evergreen bearberries alternate with dwarf birches, willows and junipers. This heathland is the most characteristic vegetation on the islands. The vegetation becomes sparser from 500 metres upwards in the increasingly alpine terrain: mosses and lichens alternate with the dwarf shrubby willows (only 2 to 6cm in height), saxifrages, types of carnation and other species.

The fauna of the Lofoten and Vesterålen is dominated, especially in the breeding season, by a large number of birds of various species such as cormorants, puffins, kittiwakes, oystercatchers, whooper swans and ptarmigans, just to name a few. Due to climate change, a dramatic decline in some seabird populations has been observed in recent years. However, the Lofoten can still boast with the world's densest population of white-tailed sea eagles. With a bit of luck you will see grey seals and common seals, as well as harbour porpoises and orcas along the coast. You will probably only see pilot whales, minke whales and dolphins on boat trips, which are offered from Stø and Andenes.

Minke whales are still being hunted off the Lofoten (a quota of about 1200 animals a year is imposed throughout Norway). Despite health concerns (heavy metals found in the meat), whaling and consumption are promoted and subsidized by the state as a valuable cultural asset. You will rarely find a party or restaurant where whale meat is not on the menu. Demands to stop whaling, outlawed internationally, are ignored by Norway.

Of the larger land mammals there are a considerable number of elks living on the Vesterålen and they have now settled in the Lofoten as well. It is impossible to miss the sheep which are to be found, especially in the Lofoten, on virtually every walk.

USEFUL TIPS

Getting there
The journey to the Lofoten and Vesterålen can be made in various ways. Whichever way you choose it can be an adventure with regards to the length of time and your experiences.

The fastest way is by plane: The central hub for reaching the islands is Oslo. From here SAS (flysas.com) and Norwegian (norwegian.com) fly to Harstad/Narvik Lufthavn, Evenes. From here Sortland on Vesterålen lies 119km away and Svolvær on the Lofoten 163km away. From Evenes you can travel on the Flybussen (airport bus; flybussen.no) to Sortland. There are various car hire firms at the airport (avinor.no/flyplass/harstad).

Another possibility is to fly with changes to Bodø with SAS or Norwegian. From Bodø travel further on with Widerøe airline (wideroe.no) to Leknes or Svolvær (Lofoten), alternatively to Stokmarknes or Andenes (Vesterålen). From Bodø, Havila kystruten (havilavoyages.com) and Hurtigruten (hurtigruten.com) offer trips on the Hurtigruten line to Stamsund, Svolvær (Lofoten) and to Stokmarknes, Sortland and Risøyhamn (Vesterålen). You can also take one of the ferries or a Hurtigbåt (torghatten-nord.no) to Røst, Værøy, Moskenes and Svolvær on the Lofoten.

By train: train enthusiasts can travel from Oslo to Trondheim and from there on to Bodø with the Nordlandsbanen (vy.no). Altogether the journey takes about 18 hours. With the Nordlandsbanen you travel across the Saltfjellet and the polar circle. Then continue your journey from Bodø as above.

From Stockholm in Sweden (sj.se) you can travel quite cheaply either directly or with one change to Narvik in Norway. The journey takes about 20 hours and goes across virtually the whole of Sweden as far as Boden and then with the Malmbanan on across the Swedish Lapland via Kiruna and Abisko. Finally, the train which is now called the Ofotbanen, runs from Riksgränsen (Sweden) to the Ofotfjorden in Narvik (Norway). From here either continue with a rental car or by bus (reisnordland.no) to the Lofoten or Vesterålen.

Driving with your own car: it's between a 1500 and 2500km drive if you start your journey from one of the ports on the Baltic Sea, depending on which ferry crossing you take and which bridges and stretches of road you choose. Here are the easiest stretches: Kiel–Oslo

A kayak trip on the Raftsundet.

(colorline.de) and continue along the E6 through Norway; also Kiel–Göteborg (stenaline.de) and continue through Sweden. All in all you need to allow at least 3 days for the trip by car from the ferry ports of Oslo, Göteborg or Trelleborg. The speed limit on country roads is between 80 and 100km/h.

Both archipelagos can be reached over land. Another possibility is to take the car ferries between Bodø and Værøy, Røst and Moskenes or the ferries between Skutvik and Svolvær, but the latter runs only in the season between 01.06. and 31.08.

Shopping

There are large supermarkets with an extensive range of goods in the main towns on the islands. There are also shopping centres in Leknes, Svolvær and Sortland. In some smaller places there are country stores with basic food stuffs on sale. Depending on which area you are in, it may be necessary for you to go a few kilometres before reaching the next shop. The prices are higher up here in Nordland than in the southern Norwegian regions. Large supermarkets are usually open Monday to Friday from 7.00 until 23.00 and Saturday until 20.00. The smaller supermarkets, country stores and other shops are mostly open until 18.00.

Ferries

If you travel to the archipelago in a motorised vehicle, you will probably use a ferry on your long journey. Numerous ferry routes, some of which are along major roads, get you across the fjords which extend inland for up to 100km, or take you to some of the islands.

More and more e-ferries have been used recently. The 'Ampere' was the first e-ferry and has crossed the Sognefjord since 2015 (E 39 between Lavik and Oppedal).

Ferry prices for vehicles up to 6m in length are reasonable, and some of the crossings are even free of charge. Ferry operators only charge for vehicles; foot passengers and passengers with a bicycle travel for free. Payment is made through electronic registration whereby the number plates are registered and an invoice, which is subject to a fee, is sent to the registered address. If you pay through FerryPay, your credit card will be charged with no extra fee (for more information on this and other payment options in English visit: autopassferje.no/en).

For timetables, check the websites of the respective ferry company or go to entur.no.

Fishing

For hundreds of years the Lofoten and also the Vesterålen have been connected to the big cod fishing industry in winter. Large schools of Northeast Arctic cod (called skrei by the Norwegians) swim at this time of year from the Barents sea down the Norwegian coast to the spawning beds. The Lofoten and in particular the warmer Vestfjorden constitute the most important and substantial spawning region. Fishermen from the whole of Norway came, and still come every year, between February and April to the archipelagos to share in this experience. In the heyday of Lofoten fishing industry up to 35,000 fishermen inhabited the archipelago and lived in the rorbuer, the fishing cabins today used by tourists.

Air-drying is the method used to preserve the huge amounts of fish that is caught. The fish is headed, gutted and hung on drying racks. This stockfish (dried cod which is called tørrfisk in Norwegian) is mostly exported to Italy. Another variation for preserving the fish is klippfisk, whereby salt is used to draw the liquid out of the fish and the result is the basis of Portuguese and Spanish bacalao dishes.

In addition to cod fishing, which is still very important for Lofoten people today, coastal fishing with smaller boats and salmon farming in aquacultures play a key role on the Vesterålen and Lofoten.

For foreigners, fishing in Norway's coastal waters is possible without a fishing licence. However, this should be done in moderation and in accordance with the rules and export regulations (!) (fiskeridir.no/English/Fishing-in-Norway/Sea-angling-in-Norway). For more information on guided fishing trips, visit the tourist office.

Internet, telecommunication

Most places offer free access to the internet. You should be aware, however, that network coverage can be sketchy on a walk. There are no roaming charges for mobile phones registered in the EU.

EMERGENCY NUMBERS

Emergency medical rescue: 113
Doctor: 116 117
Fire service: 110
Police: 112
Emergency app: Hjelp 113
Breakdown Service Falck: 02 222
Breakdown Service Viking: 06 000

Rorbuer, camping, hotels and other accommodation

The most popular types of accommodation are the so-called rorbuer, former fishermens' cabins where fishermen used to stay overnight in basic conditions during the winter fishing season. The rorbuer are these days rustic, but some are furnished with all modern comforts. They are, according to their purpose, located in authentic surroundings by the water.
Sleeping arrangements are usually bunk beds, frequently also simple beds or mattresses in lofts (hems). Simple small 2 bed rorbuer cost from 800 NOK per night. The more people sleep in the rorbuer, the lower the price per person. In some places you will also find accommodation in fishermen's houses where you can rent individual rooms.

The sky is full of torsk (cod): dried fish is the no. 1 export of the Lofoten.

LEISURE TIME AND SPORT

Art
There are, on the Lofoten especially, a few galleries; Kaare Espolin Johnson, Dagfinn Bakke, Eva Harr, Ola Strand and others. You will often come across street art, the most famous being the artwork of Dolk and Pøbel, which is already fading.

Climbing
A climbing and boulder paradise can be found at Henningsvær and Kalle on the Lofoten: the finest granite climbing with a fantastic backdrop of the sea.

Diving
Snorkelling and diving experiences into the underwater world of the Lofoten are really something quite special: lofoten-diving.com (Ballstad); lofoten-opplevelser.no (Henningsvaer, snorkelling only).

Fishing
See the Fishing section on page 28.

Golf
Tee off around midnight with views of the sea and sun. The Lofoten Golf Link on Gimsøy lies directly on the Norwegian Sea, one of the most northerly located golf courses in the world (lofotenlinks.no).

Horseriding
Horse riding tours can be arranged on the island of Vestvågøya (hovhestegard.no and lofothest.no).

Museums
Larger museums worth visiting are the Lofotr Viking Museum in Borg (lofotr.no), the Norwegian Fishing Village Museum and the Lofoten Stockfish Museum in Å, the complex in Storvågen at Kabelvåg and the Hurtigruten Museum in Stokmarknes. Other museums are mentioned in some of the walks under Tip (visitlofoten.com, lofoten-info.no, museumnord.no, visitvesteralen.no).

Skulpturlandskap Nordland
The art project of international artists in the Nordland communities includes, amongst others, Mannen fra Havet in Bø, the mirror between Rørvik and the Gimsøystraumbrua bridge and the Øymuseet in Andenes (skulpturlandskap.no).

Sami culture
The Inga Sami Siida farm in the vicinity of Sortland breeds reindeers

and offers tours and other events to do with the Sami culture (inga-samisiida.no).

Sea kayaking
Sea kayaks can be rented on both the Lofoten and Vesterålen (addresses below). For this you will need a so-called våtkart which corresponds to the European paddle pass EPP2 respectively BCU 2Star. Otherwise there are opportunities to join a guided kayak tour – in Reine and the surrounding area at reineadventure.com, reinefjord.no, sagaadventureslofoten.com, in Ballstad at lofoten-diving.com, in Kabelvåg at lofoten-aktiv.no; on Vesterålen at vpks.no and in Ringstad yttersiden.no.

Surfing, SUP, kites etc.
Northern Norway's surfing paradise lies in Unstad. The highest waves, of course, occur in winter when the surrounding mountains are covered in snow. You can book classes in Unstad and hire equipment (unstadarcticsurf.com, lofotensurfsenter.no and lofotenadventure.co). Other courses and the hire of equipment is also offered by lofoten-beachcamp.no in Flakstad on the Skagen beach.

Swimming
The sandy beaches on the Lofoten and Vesterålen are exceptionally beautiful in any weather – equally Caribbean and Nordic. Some of the loveliest on the Lofoten are Bunesstranda, Kvalvika, Ramberg, Haukland and Rørvik. On Vesterålen the most beautiful beaches are to be found in the community of Bø, in Stø, in Bleik and also Andenes.

Whale Watching
Whale watching tours are on offer from the little harbour town of Stø (arcticwhaletours.no) and from Andenes (seasafariandenes.no and whalesafari.no), both in the Vesterålen.

Campsites are the cheapest places to spend the night. The sites are usually nicely laid out and offer adequate space for your tent or your camper. Comfort can vary from very basic to good. The individual sites cost from 200 NOK upwards. There are usually small kitchens and recreation rooms on site, as well as WLAN. You can also rent smallish or larger cabins on most of the campsites. The most basic 2 person cabins cost from 500 NOK upwards.

There are youth hostels (vandrerhjem) in the Lofoten in Å, Ballstad and Kabelvåg and also on Vesterålen in Andenes.

There are hotels in the main towns of the islands and also holiday homes, B&Bs and seasonal hostels. You will find suggestions for every taste at lofoten.info and visitvesteralen.no.

Languages and spelling

Norway has two main dialects of the official language: bokmål (used by 88% of the population) and nynorsk (used by 12% of the population) as well as the three Sami languages of nordsamisk, lulesamisk and sørsamisk. Bokmål has its roots in Danish and is the Norwegian version of it, while nynorsk is mainly based on rural Norwegian dialects. In addition to these standardised and repeatedly reformed written languages, there are various dialects.

The municipalities (kommune) as well as school districts decide which written language applies to their area. In 25% of the municipalities (mainly in western Norway which is home to 12% of the population), nynorsk is the

The Sakrisøy rorbuer stands in front of a heavenly backdrop.

View of the Flakstadpollen.

official language, while 33% use bokmål and the rest of the municipalities are neutral. All this doesn't make it easier to understand the Norwegian languages, especially as the written and spoken word often differ greatly from each other.
The official spelling Statens Kartverk uses on their maps and signs depends on which written language is used locally. The respective language is used by internet search engines, information portals and brochures as well as the DNT. This guide follows the same procedure (deviations are indicated, where appropriate).

Tourist offices
The tourist associations of the Lofoten and Vesterålen produce information leaflets in English and their website can also be accessed in English: lofoten.info, lofoten-info.no and visitvesteralen.no.
Further information, details and weather forecasts are available from tourist offices in Moskenes, Leknes, Svolvær as well as in Sortland and Andenes.

Traffic
The optimum mode of travel is by car. The road network of both archipelagos is very well-developed and almost completely surfaced. There are petrol stations in the important places. You can reach the Lofoten as well

as Vesterålen without having to take a ferry. Since 2007 this is possible via the Lofast (Lofotens fastlandsforbindelse) onto Lofoten. The main islands of the archipelago are connected by bridges and tunnels. Between Fiskebøl and Melbu there's a regular ferry service so that you can travel from the Lofoten to Vesterålen without much of a detour.

On some walks it's a good idea to use a bike for the return stretch from your destination to the start.

The island of Skrova is reachable by ferry from Svolvær and the islands of Værøy and Røst from Moskenes or Bodø. From Andenes you can reach the island of Senja also by ferry (senjafergene.no).

You can find timetables at torghatten-nord.no, and the times of the Hurtigruten line at hurtigruten.com and havilavoyages.com. Public transport by bus is an interurban service with low frequency at times. There are timetables online at reisnordland.no.

The national online travel planer entour.no (also available as app) lists all public transport connections – bus, rail, boat – between start and finish, including all stops and transfer stations. All public transport tickets can be purchased via this portal since November 2024.

Cars can be rented at the airports from well-known rental companies. Up-to-date information about local rental companies can be found online if you search for Leiebil Lofoten or Vesterålen.

Method of payment

Cashless payments are common practice in Norway, you rarely need cash. There are cash machines at banks in the larger towns or at supermarkets. It's not possible to change money locally.

Customs regulations

The current customs regulations can be found under toll.no. You can find all the necessary information under 'Travelling'. The regulations for the import of alcohol and food and the export of caught fish are important.

SHORT WALKING GLOSSARY

Norwegian	English
bekk, -en	creek
berg, -et	mountain
botn, -en	end of the inner valley, end of the fjord
bre, -en	glacier
bro, -a/bru, -a	bridge
bu, -a	hut
bukt, -a	bay
by, -en	town
dal, -en	valley
egg, -en	ridge
eid, -et	isthmus
elv, -a	river
fare, -en	danger
ferge, -a/ferje, -a	ferry
fjell, -et	mountain area above treeline
fly, -a/-en	high plateau
fonn, -a/-en	firn
foss, -en	waterfall
fylke, -et	province (district)
fyr, -et	lighthouse
gjel, -et	gorge
grotte, -a/-en	grotto
haug, -en	hill
hav, -et	sea, ocean
hei, -a/-en	high grass-covered plateau
hjelp, -en	help
hole, -a/-en	cave
hule, -a/-en	cave
holm/holme, -en	skerry, islet
hytte, -a/-en	cabin, hut, mountain hotel
hø, -a/-en	crest
høgd, -a/høyde,-en	height, mountain range
is, -en	ice
juv, -et	canyon
kommune	community
kyst, -en	coast
midnattssoll, -a/-en	midnight sun
myr, -a/-en	mire, bog, fen
nasjonalpark, -en	national park
nykkel, -en	key
nøkkel, -en	key
ras, -et	avalanche
regn, -et	rain
rygg, -en	ridge
seter, -a/-en	alpine pasture
sjø, -en	sea, lake
skar, -et/skard,-et	saddle
skog, -en/skau, -en	wood, forest
snø, -en	snow
sol, -a/-en	sun
sti, -en	path
strand, -a/-en	beach
støl, -en	alpine pasture/hut
telt, -et	tent
tid, -a/-en	time
time, -en	hour
tind, -en	summit
tjørn, -a/tjern, -et	tarn
topp, -a/-en	top
tur, -en	tour
ur, -a/-en/urd, -a	scree
utsikt, -a/-en	view
vann, -et/vatn, -et	lake (water)
varde, -en	cairn
veg, -en/vei, -en	road, track, path
vidde, -a/-en	high plateau
vær, -et	weather
øy, -a/-en	island
å, -a/-en	little stream
bratt	steep
farlig/farleg	dangerous
forbudt/forby	prohibited
full	full
gå	go
krevende	demanding
ledig	free
lille/litle	small
nedre/nedra	lower
nord	north
nordlig/nordleg	northern
stengt	closed
stor	large
sør, søre/søndre	south, southern
ut	out
vandre/vandra	hike
vest, vestre	west, western
øst/aust	east
østre/austre	eastern
øvre	upper
åpen/open	open

Walking on the Lofoten

The Lofoten (old Norwegian for 'lynx foot') are off the north Norwegian coast and separated from the mainland by the 100km wide and 700m deep Vestfjorden. They extend north of the polar circle at a length of 150km from the southwest to the northeast between the 67th and 68th line of latitude. The Lofoten in the northeast border directly on Vesterålen while the Norwegian Sea (Norskehavet) extends beyond to the north and to the west. The archipelago consists of over 80 larger islands and thousands of skerries. The most important islands are Røstlandet, Værøy, Moskenesøya, Flakstadøya, Vestvågøya, Gimsøya, Austvågøya, Skrova, Litlmolla and Stormolla.

Fish drying racks are everywhere on the Lofoten and you'll find the stockfish (tørrfisk) hanging on these racks until June. It's all about the fish here, and not only in the winter months when the big cod fishing takes place. Lofoteners live from and with the sea.

With the exception of Røstlandet, the islands consist of steeply towering peaks and mountain chains, some of which have an alpine character. Boggy plateaus, lakes and both rugged and beautiful beach sections of the coast offer attractive walks for the hiker.

View from Værøy of Mosken island.

Municipality of Røst: 'The fish in the seas are our daily bread...' (Petter Dass)

The municipality of Røst lies far out to sea and with its 365 islands forms the southwestern foothills of the Lofoten. The main island of Røstlandet rises only a few metres above sea level (Walk 1). Southwest of the inhabited main island, however, several colossal and steep islands tower up from the sea, the most famous of which are the bird islands of Trenyken (with the reputed three-summit mountain of the same name), Vedøya, Storfjellet and Nykene. Together with almost 600 people on Røst living from fishing, the island municiplaity hosts the largest bird colony in Norway.

Walk 1 in this guide book invites you to explore Røstlandet in a leisurely fashion and gives you the feeling of being really far away from the hustle and bustle of civilization.

Municipality of Værøy: the smallest Lofoten municipality

The municipality of Værøy borders the municipality of Røst to the northeast. It consists of the larger island of Værøy and the uninhabited island of Mosken both of which rise steeply up out of the sea. The mountain range on Værøy towers up like a curved wall between the Vestfjorden and the Norwegian Sea and its peaks reach heights of over 400m – a fascinating area to go for a hike (Walks 2 and 3). Like the people of Røst, the almost 750 inhabitants of Værøy live mainly from fishing. Måstad (Walk 2) played an important role until the middle of the last century. It became famous for its puffin colony and Lunde dogs.

North of the island of Mosken lies the Moskstraumen, one of the most powerful tidal currents in the world, also known as the Maelstrom. It is 4 to 5km wide and only 40 to 60m deep. The whirlpools and rapids created by it have always misled strangers into excessive exaggeration – while the local residents accepted it as a phenomenon to be treated with respect. The mythological background can be found in the Song of Grótti, an old Norse poem, from the Poetic Edda. There are also more modern literary immortalisations by Edgar Allen Poe ('A Descent into the Maelstrom'), Jules Verne ('Twenty Thousand Leagues Under the Sea') and other authors.

Municipality of Moskenes: where the Lofoten are the most monumental

The municipality of Moskenes is located on the southern part of Moskenesøya Island. The population of 1100 inhabitants who live predominantly from the fishing industry and from tourism now only exists along the coast of the Vestfjorden. Until the middle of the last century there were settlements on the Lofotodden (the southern tip of Moskenesøya) and on the northwestern outer edge of the island. Due to the motorisation of fishing boats and the impossibility of expanding the necessary ports the settlements were abandoned.

Today's villages cling to the high cliffs and small islets along the coastline like swallows' nests. Protected by the mighty peaks beyond you can enjoy the sun's rays from Å to Reine more regularly than on the Norwegian Sea coast which although littered with sandy beaches, is sometimes difficult to reach. While hiking in the municipality of Moskenes (Walks 4 to 7) you walk across rock strata that are billions of years old and discover some of the most spectacular views yet always remain close to the element of water – the sea, the island's deep and dramatic fjords and a myriad of glacial lakes. The town of Sørvågen has special historical significance. It was here that in 1861 Norway's first fishing telegraph came into operation and in 1906 the first wireless telegraph line in northern Europe was installed. This was thanks to cod fishing – faster information about the catch enabled better marketing.

Municipality of Flakstad: pleasant coastal walks and delightful bays

The municipality is located on both the island of Flakstadøya and the northern part of Moskenesøya. Most people live here along the outer edge of the islands. The agricultural land is larger than in the municipality of Moskenes which is characterised by rugged cliffs. Free-grazing sheep are to be found everywhere here all through summer. Even so, everything revolves around the fish here too.

Exposed to the elements of the sea: the village of Vikten with its beach and Bjørntinden.

The Reinebringen massif, Moskenesøya.

On the island of Flakstadøya, which is divided into three 'ribs', the mountain ranges stretch from north to south with peaks reaching heights of up to 934m. On the walks (Walks 8 to 18) you can expect beautiful panoramas and glacial landscapes as well as varied coastal paths with idyllic fishing villages and enchanting white beaches. The old bunkers in the Skjelfjorden – the small 'Norwegian Scapa Flow' – help to keep the history of World War II alive.

Municipality of Vestvågøy: with reminders of Viking life

The most populous municipality of Lofoten with more than 11,000 inhabitants is the main island of Vestvågøya which is characterised by a central core and many smaller peninsulas. High, and at times jagged peaks dominate the outer areas while the heartland is dominated by a gentler mountain range and large agricultural areas – a picture that one is not used to on other Lofoten islands.

The municipality of Vestvågøy is one of the largest agricultural municipalities north of the Arctic Circle. So it's no wonder that two families, Aalan Gård and Lofoten Gårdsysteri, invite you to a new culinary experience with

The Viking Museum in Borg on Vestvågøya.

the cheese production on their farms. Fishing sets the tone once again in Ballstad and Stamsund on the Vestfjorden. Not far from Leknes a replica has been made of the largest longhouse of a chieftain ever found in Norway. In the Lofotr Viking Museum you can experience the Viking Age as it really was for Lofoten ancestors and spend many interesting hours here.
Hiking on Vestvågøya (Walks 19 to 30) has something for everyone: from strenuous mountain walks to easy short excursions along the coastline or over gentle hills, fantastic views across the water and the land, and also the fascination of the Norwegian Sea lit by the midnight sun. Most walks on the otherwise bustling island take you to places of complete solitude where you can just stand and enjoy.

Municipality of Vågan: summits as far as the eye can see

The municipality of Vågan consists of several large islands and parts of islands. These include: Gimsøya, the central and southern part of Austvågøya (the border is south of the Grunnførfjorden, the hamlet of Higrav, and south of Trollfjorden), the southeastern tip of Hinnøya, Skrova, Litlmolla and Stormolla. In the north the municipality of Hadsel (Vesterålen) borders on Vågan and in the east the municipality of Lødingen.

The origins of the administrative division of the islands between the Lofoten and Vesterålen stem from the times when there were no roads or tracks in the regions. Routes that are easy to use today were unthinkable in the past and so the boat determined the orientation of regional borders. A strong loyalty to these borders persists to this day. No inhabitants of Fiskebøl would ever have the idea of calling themselves Lofotinger. Accordingly, the highlight of Trollfjorden that the Lofoten like to advertise is, in fact, a treasure belonging to the Vesterålers.

Like the southern Lofoten, the municipality of Vågan has little space for agricultural land. The localities, with a few exceptions, all lie on the water and are dominated by smallish and larger ports, shipyards and the fish processing industry. The municipal centre in Svolvær is also the capital of the entire archipelago and is, despite it only having 4,500 inhabitants, a vibrant 'metropolis' where there is virtually everything on hand and where everyone meets. The smaller and historically more important places worth seeing are the much more leisurely Kabelvåg and Henningsvær.

Our selected walks 31 to 42 offer a wide range of the most pleasant hikes in this area, from easy ascents to challenging full-day tours. They go sometimes more, sometimes less strenuously uphill, but each time you will be rewarded with beautiful panoramas.

View of Rulten and Austnesfjorden from Geitgallien.

1 Røstlandet

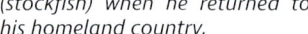

Paradise at the furthest point on the Lofoten

If you like remoteness and simplicity, this is the place to be 100 kilometres west of Bodø, in the middle of the polar sea. The islands of the municipality of Røst are the northernmost region of the world where the annual average temperatures do not fall below 0 °C – ideal conditions for cod drying. And this is where the story began for this successful export business. In January 1432, the Venetian nobleman Pietro Querini was stranded with ten other sailors on Sandøya, south of Røstlandet, after a shipwreck and weeks of drifting along the Norwegian coast. He was a guest and observer of the people of Røst until May and he became the first exporter of 'stoccafisso'

(stockfish) when he returned to his homeland country.

Italy is still the largest consumer of stockfish from the Lofoten and in particular from Røst and the municipality has maintained very friendly ties with its twin town of Sandrigo in Veneto to this day. The 'Querinifesten' (Querini festival) takes place every year at the beginning of August in honour of Querini. The absolute highlight of the festival is, without doubt, the Querini opera which has been performed three times up to now by both laymen and professional artists.

The 365 islands and skerries of the municipality are home to nearly 530 people and many sheep, but also to the largest bird breeding colonies on the European mainland. For reasons of nature conservancy and species protection issues this diverse ornithological world is now under protection, especially as there has been a massive decrease in population in places in recent years. The population of puffins in particular declined, from 1.5 million to 325,000 pairs in 2017, due to the decimated stock of their food sources. In honour of this beautiful bird, the Lunde festival takes place every year in the last week of June. The large variety of seabirds and waders encouraged conservationists in the 1930s to introduce a group of king and macaroni penguins on Røst as well as Gjesvær in Finnmark. The nowadays unthinkable experiment went badly wrong and the last wild penguin in the Northern Hemisphere was spotted probably in 1954.

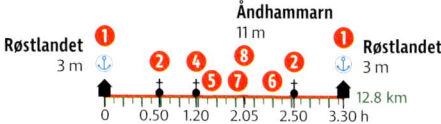

Starting point: Røstlandet, ferry dock, 3m.
Grade: easy walk on surfaced roads and over boggy marshland.
Infrastructure: various possibilities for accommodation, restaurant, petrol station and supermarket on Røstlandet.
Alternatives: You can shorten the walk by using a bike or a car which you can park at the bell tower ❺. From here you start walking in the direction of Åndhammarn und Ystøran.
Tips: at the car park by the ferry dock you will find a small tourist information office; rost.kommune.no (only in Norwegian).

Cycle hire and visit to the on-site stockfish warehouse at the Røst Bryggehotell. Boat trips from the harbour into the archipelago of Røst are on offer during high season.
Small art galleries, Kulturlandskap (sculpture in the landscape) 'Il Nido' (the nest) by Luciano Fabro on the island of Vedøya, the Lundefestivalen (lundefestivalen.no) in the last week of June and the Querini festivals at the beginning of August (querini.no) bring a fair amount of culture into the otherwise quiet archipelago.
Map: Vest-Lofoten.

Start your walk directly at the ferry dock on **Røstlandet** ❶. Walk northeastwards along the Fv 7582 and negotiate your way across small islands and parts of islands that are connected to one another by bridges and dams. The island is flat as far as you can see. The huge mountain peaks that you can make out, in the southwest and east especially, belong to other

Left: view of Åndhammarn – the highest rise on Røstlandet.
Below: view across the eastern side of Røstlandet with Stavøya peak.

islands of the archipelago, for example, Storfjellet, Vedøya and the famous and iconic island of Trenyken which is recognisable from miles around. These islands are only reachable by boat. In good weather you can also see as far as the islands of Værøy, Mosken and Moskenesøya to the northeast.

80m after the ferry dock on the left hand side of the road you can pay a visit to the small tourist office while next to the Røst Bryggehotell, there is a small gallery exhibiting nature photos. The art collection is housed in a 100 year old house which is also well worth seeing. Further along the route you come past restaurants, cafés and bars, places to stay and other galleries. The widely spread buildings allow you open views of the countryside with colourful wooden houses liying higgledy-piggledy inbetween meadows, bogs, lakes and wooden fish drying racks.

After 1.2km from your starting point the road goes round a right hand bend. Follow this and after another 1.4km you come to a **church** ❷ which was consecrated in 1900. Inside you will find one of five triptychs dating back to the early 16th century which were donated by Princess Isabella of Austria, the later wife of Christian II and thus Queen of Norway, in gratitude for her rescue from a stormy sea crossing. The church stands in the social and political centre of the Røst community. It has a town hall, school with a swimming pool (50 children in classes 1–10), nursery school (places for 18 children up to 6 years old), library, police station, doctor's, care home, Querini sports' hall and the island's own radio station.

Gammelkirka.

As you continue along your way the distinctive summit of the island Stavøya is getting closer and closer. The built-up area starts to retreat and the landscape opens out until you soon have a completely clear view of this 140m high elevation.

After a gentle S-bend and a total of 3.7km turn left away from the Fv 7582 onto a narrow road, the **Markveien** ❸. There are no signposts or waymarkers so it's best to orientate yourself along beside a small elongated lake on your right. There are two white houses on your left and the Markveien turns off left between them. After a few metres you can already see your next destination in the middle of an area of pasture on the right hand side – the ruins of Røstlandet church dating back to 1839. But first of all walk 500m to a cattle grid. There's a small information board here on the right hand side which shows the start of the path to the ruins of the old church, which you can reach easily via a 500m-long path.

The **Gammelkirka** ❹ – the 'old church' – was designed by the renowned architect Hans D.F. von Linstow who also designed the royal palace in Oslo. Von Linstow was commissioned to draw up plans for new country churches. However, his plan was somewhat misinterpreted on Røst: the outside measurements were switched with the inside measurements and the church in the end was smaller than intended with only 78 seats. Consequently the Gammelkirka only stood from 1839 to 1900 before, according to the wishes of the community, it was replaced with the church that still stands today. It was mostly demolished and the contents of the interior sold off by auction on the island. The fact that the church was made of stone is unusual for rural areas and presumably was due to the fact that its predecessor was destroyed by a hurricane.

You will still find puffins ('lundefugl') all over the place on Røst!

Walk back along the path to the road and continue in the direction of the next curiosity – the already visible bell tower of a church built in 1825, but already destroyed in 1835. The tower was preserved and today it stands in the medieval churchyard and, amongst other things, serves as an orientation point for sailors. After 200m you will have reached the **bell tower** ❺. At this point you also meet the Fv 7586 where you turn right and continue walking in the direction of the airport.

Barely 400m further on you come past the community road maintenance depot and the **fire station** ❻ (Miljøstasjon and Brannstasjon). Immediately after the fire station turn off left and continue along between the fire station and the airport fence. You are now walking through a bird protection zone where you are asked to proceed with extreme caution and awareness during the breeding season. Therefore do not take the clearly visible path along by the fence, but turn slightly to the left onto a less used path. This leads you round a bend, at first southwards and after a few metres westwards, where you can see Badetjønna lake as far as the remains of a circular wall. With all probability this was to do with the boundary of one of the oldest church squares on Røst dating back to pre 1536. Archaeological digs have discovered remains of small wooden crosses which are unique to Norway.

Continue along the path until you reach the southern corner of the airport fencing. Shortly afterwards you come to a crossroads with a signpost to Åndhammarn (Ånghammaren), your next destination. Walk northwestwards past the airport complex and between the marshy lakes as far as the highest elevation on Røstlandet. But before 'walking up' Åndhammarn you come to a **crossroads** ❼. Reaching the highest point of Røstlandet sometimes requires skipping across the rocks, depending on the water level. From the top of **Åndhammarn** ❽, you can see the row of islands which you will explore if you opt for Alternative 1 of this walk. Go back to the **crossroads** ❼ where you have two options to continue: if you go left, you get to Ystøran (Alternative 1); if you go right, you walk back to the ferry dock via Ystnes (Alternative 2). Walk back to the **fire station** ❻ along the same path. From here, continue along the Fv 7586 which after 1.1km takes you to the **church** ❷ at the village centre. Turn right here and return to the **starting point** ❶.

Alternative 1: Continuation of the walk to **Ystøran** and back (1 hr, a 'blue' walk)

The walk from the **crossroads** ❼ to Ystøran can only be undertaken if the water level is low (low tide). Turn northeastwards and walk for about 500m across the marshland parallel to the airport runway. After you have left the marsh lakes behind continue left, northwestwards, until you come to some stone causeways which lead you, without getting your feet wet, to the skerry of Heimstøran. Turn west here and a gentle stroll brings you across some more causeways and tiny islands to the outermost island of **Ystøran**.

Alternative 2: return from the **crossroads** ❼ via **Ystnes** and the Fv 7584 (45 minutes to the ferry dock, a 'blue' walk)

If you are on foot, you can return from the **crossroads** ❼ a different way in the direction of **Ystnes**. For 1.5km the route goes across boggy and marshy land and past cod drying racks. You meet the Fv 7584 in Ystnes; turn left here and after just over 500m reach the Fv 7582. Now turn to the right and walk back to the ferry dock on **Røstlandet** ❶.

Røstlandet ferry mooring and the islands of Vedøya, Storfjellet and Treniken.

↗ 680m | ↘ 680m | 15.0km
5.45 hrs

2 Måstad and Måstadheia, 407m

Walk to the former bird paradise

An enchanting coastal and mountain walk to the abandoned hamlet of Måstad and onto Måstadheia located above. Once there were 150 people in Måstad living from fishing, sheep rearing and the hunting of birds and collecting birds' eggs. The fish beds were abundant, the grazing pastures luxuriant and succulent and in order to catch the puffins the women and children deployed a special breed of dog – the Norwegian Lunde dog. However, the arrival of motorised fishing boats and the unsuccessful connection to Værøy's road and electricity network spelt the end of the settlement. The last permanent resident left Måstad in 1974 and the era of a completely unique settlement came to an end. Tens of thousands of puffins (lundefugl) used to graze on the slopes of the Måstadheia until recently, but their population has disintegrated due to the lack of food.

The abandoned settlement of Måstad.

The cemetery in Nordland on Værøy.

Starting point: Nordlandshagen, car park (with toilets), 15m. Follow the road west of Nordland for 2.5km past the former Værøy airport, at the end along a gravel track.
Grade: waymarked footpath as far as Måstad, loamy sections on meadow slopes and many sections of scree along the coast, surefootedness and a good head for heights is needed on the ascent onto Måstadheia.
Infrastructure: accommodation, restaurant, supermarket and petrol station in Sørland.
Alternative: if you turn south on the col ❹ you will reach the summit of Måhornet (439m) after an ascent of 170 vertical metres.
Tip: the oldest church on the Lofoten is located in Nordland (1714) with an altar of historical interest whose alabaster figures date back to the 15th century.
Map: Vest-Lofoten.

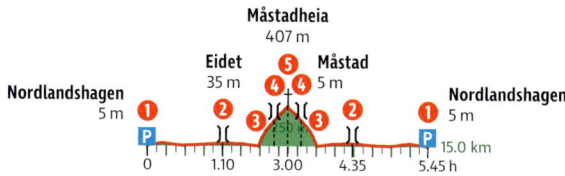

On the way to Måstad.

From **Nordlandshagen** ❶ walk along the roadway in a southwesterly direction, parallel to the old power lines. In the 1950s an attempt was made to connect Måstad with a road to Nordland, but it was prevented by repeatedly falling scree. Consequently the old roadway soon disappears and you ascend and descend along the coastline over a varied terrain of meadows, hillsides and scree slopes. The old power line aids your orientation and there are also red dots along the way. The vertical wall of Håen rises up on the left hand side and right on the top you can see a radar station. Suddenly the old raised causeway begins again and you reach a large meadow area. Follow the path southwards over the **Eidet pass** ❷ and in so doing, change from the outer edge of Værøy on the Norwegian Sea to the inner edge on the Vestfjorden. You now find yourself standing before the impressive bay of Måstadvika. The old road winds its way along beside the rock wall above the bay and you can soon see the white sandy beach of Sanden to the north of you where the Repphellaren cave is located in which 3000 year old rock paintings have been discovered. The path brings you further on to the abandoned settlement of Måstad whose few remaining buildings are used as summer houses by the descendants of former inhabitants. At the end of **Måstad** ❸ there is a sign pointing the way to the local water source.

In order to hike up to Måstadheia ascend the steep path zigzagging up the prominent mountain spine and after that walk across the entire mountainside to the **col** ❹ above Måstad. From here you have the option of climbing up to the left onto the summit of Måhornet, 439m (170 vertical metres, 40 minutes).

Turn right along the clearly defined path and eventually reach the large meadowed plateau of **Måstadheia** ❺. From here at the top you are afforded a fascinating panorama across Værøy. In the southwest you can see the islands of Røst scattered in the Norwegian Sea and on the northeastern horizon the enormous towering wall of rock faces of the other Lofoten islands. On the mountain slope below you there was, until a few years ago, a large colony of puffins. You can still watch the activities of these beautiful birds from here, but you will need plenty of patience and luck. For those who are absolutely free of vertigo there is the possible continuation of the path along the narrow grassy ridge in the direction of Breidfjellet, 397m.

Return to **Nordlandshagen** ❶ the same way.

↗ 430m | ↘ 430m | 4.8km
2.00 hrs

3 Håen, 438m

To the north atlantic sentry post

This summit is also called NATO-Toppen by the locals on account of the radar station. Even so, it offers a beautiful 360 degree panorama of Værøy and its surroundings, and especially distant views across the Måstadheia and Måhornet mountain ranges all the way down to Måstadvika and Sanden.

Starting point: Marka, car park, 19m. From the ferry dock in Værøy drive along the Fv 7588 to Sørland. After 2.5km turn off left before the municipal administration. After about 2km, shortly before the end of the road, you will see on the right hand side a transformer station and blue agricultural buildings; park here on the gravel square.
Grade: relatively easy walk, but care should be taken on the ridge and the descent is steep and stony.
Infrastructure: accommodation, restaurant, supermarket and petrol station in Sørland.
Alternative: ascent from Norlandshagen over Hornet (45 mins as far as the col ❷, a 'red walk', a steep, stony path on the ascent): from Nordlandshagen follow the first few metres of the route to Måstad and start climbing into the slope of Hornet. The ascent continues steeply up the grassy slope and in the higher areas, over scree, at times slippery, until you reach the col ahead. From there it's steeply uphill to the right to the summit of Hornet, 346m, then descend southwestwards to the col ❷ which is mentioned in the main route.
Tip: A trip to the outer side of Værøy facing the Norwegian Sea and to the village of Nordland with the oldest church on the Lofoten is well worth it. In the church there's an altar of historical interest with alabaster figures from the 15th century.
Map: Vest-Lofoten.

Junction of paths on the col.

The Måstadfjellet mountain range.

From the car park in **Marka** ❶ take the clear path (behind the blue hall) which zigzags up the hillside in a northerly direction across meadows. Cross the asphalt road several times which is closed to public traffic and leads onto the summit and to the radar station. After the last hairpin bend the footpath forks off to the right and leads in a straight line onto the **col** ❷ from where your view drops steeply down to the Norwegian Sea. The path ascends on the left hand side continuing along the ridge with views of the steep northern slope of the Håen. You can now see the military installations located on the summit. As you continue along the ridge the Håheia meadows extend on your left at the end of which you meet the approach road again. From here continue to the summit of **Håen** ❸ where you are afforded a magnificent view of Måstadvika bay.

For your return, walk at first downhill on the asphalt road and then, at the first bend, take the path branching off right here that leads steeply down across meadows and scree slopes back to **Marka** ❶. Alternatively you can return by descending the same way you came up.

TOP 4

Munkebu, 405m

↗ 750m | ↘ 750m | 9.9km
4.30 hrs

Into the alpine heart of Moskenesøya

This varied walk brings you to waterfalls, so-called paternoster lakes and into alpine country with sharp mountain peaks – it's worth taking the whole day for this walk in the heart of Moskenesøya island.

Starting point: Sørvågen, paid car park on the western side of Sørvågvatnet lake, 21m. Shortly after the modern school complex in Sørvågen turn off right and follow the road to the end. An alternative paid car park can be found opposite the school on the E 10.
Grade: moderate walk, rocky sections with chains for protection, some cairns and coloured waymarkers. Large boggy sections.
Infrastructure: accommodation and restaurants in Sørvågen and Å. Supermarket in Sørvågen and Reine, petrol station in Reine. The locked and unstaffed Munkebu hut is only available to members of the DNT (lofoten-turlag.no).
Linking tip: you can extend this walk by making an ascent of Hermannsdalstinden (Walk 5) and Munkan (see Alternative).
Tips: in Å there's the Norwegian Fishing Village Museum and a Lofoten Stockfish Museum. In the latter you can learn all there is to know about the Lofoten's 'gold'. The (small) Norwegian Telecommunications Museum can be found in Sørvågen.
Map: Vest-Lofoten.

From the car park in **Sørvågen** ❶ start your walk along the gravel path that runs along the broad ridge between the lakes of Tindsvatnet and Sørvågvatnet. At the end of the path you come over a rocky hillock (parallel to the power line) to the Stuvdalselva waterfalls which are at their most impressive in early summer. Cross the stream over a bridge and after that ascend a small incline. The path brings you along the right hand side of Stuvdalsvatnet (reservoir for drink-

Waterfalls at Stuvdalselva.

ing water). This lake has, considering its size, an extraordinary depth of 127m. A layer of primeval seawater lies at the bottom. At the northeastern end of **Stuvdalsvatnet** ❷ walk around the small Badevika bay and follow the signpost for 'Munkebu'.

A little later, the path ascends steeply, with a chain for protection, over a bar of rock that has been polished smooth by glacial ice. Then continue your walk across the slightly sloping incline above Tridalsvatnet lake and soon you will see an elongated boggy area with countless small lakes ahead of you. After that negotiate the next high step; there are several paths here, but a few cairns help you with the route finding. From the path you have a great view of Fjerddalsvatnet lake a long way down to the left. The path now continues in a northeasterly direction onto a **col** ❸. Merraflestinden, 537m, rises up ahead on the right. Keep ascending on the left across a grassy hillside while below you can see the Djupfjorden with its elegant road bridge. Now you come past the elevation of Djupfjordheia, 510m, on your right. The **Munkebu hut** ❹ is surrounded by lakes and

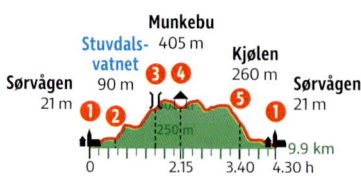

Sørvågen, with the lakes of Tindsvatnet, Stuvdalsvatnet, Tridalsvatnet and Fjerddalsvatnet.

high mountains and lies in a valley basin into which you descend. At an altitude of 400m the terrain has an alpine feel to it and provides you with countless possiblities for further walks and exploration.

For your way back choose the path across the western flank of Merraflestinden. First, walk back over the Djupfjordheia, from where you can already see your destination. First descend onto the **col ❸**, but do not take the path to the right (your outward route), take instead the clearly visible track towards the mountain hillside. There is also the option of walking along the edge of the ridge across the summit of the 537m-high Merraflestinden. Otherwise keep following the path across the western flank. The path gently ascends and leads as far as a broad ridge. From here, we walk leisurely through heathland covered in dwarf shrubs until the path descends steeply to **Kjølen col ❺**. Once you have arrived there you need to overcome a steep section, well-worn in places, but boggy and laborious, down to **Stuvdalsvatnet lake ❷**. Here you meet the path you ascended on your outward route up to the Munkebu hut, and return back to **Sørvågen ❶**.

Alternative: from the Munkebu hut onto the summit of Munkan, 775m (1.30 hrs, 370 vertical metres, a 'red' walk; occasional cairns)
This path starts from the **Munkebu** ❹ and runs the first few metres round the left hand side of the lake. The path is clearly visible and well-trodden, mostly up a steady steep incline interspersed with stones. Already on the first few metres of ascent you are afforded a lovely view looking back which, as you climb higher and higher, quickly opens out. Very soon you are looking down on the lakes of Tennesvatnet and Krokvatnet. You are surrounded by alpine-type peaks and the 1029m high Hermannsdalstinden towers up opposite. At an altitude of 591m you are surprised to see a small art installation a short way off the path – a great place to sit for a while and contemplate your thoughts. As you continue on your way you pass a small mountain lake lying on your right. Once you've reached the summit of **Munkan** you find yourself on a plateau dotted with cairns. The all-encompassing view of the mountain and fjord landscape as well as the Norwegian Sea and the Vestfjorden gives you the feeling of being on top of the world.
To **return** to the hut, choose the same path, but be careful to climb a small rock step to the right above the mountain lake taking you back to the Munkebu hut. If you want to go directly to **Djupfjordheia**, take a short cut along the path.

Munkebu hut with Munkan in the background.

↗ 1570m | ↘ 1570m | 13.7km
8.00 hrs

5 Hermannsdalstinden, 1029m

On the highest mountain of Moskenesøya

This walk to the highest summit of Moskenesøya brings you into alpine terrain after only a few vertical metres of ascent. A landscape that has been shaped by glaciers with smoothly polished rocks, lakes and fjords, lies at the foot of Hermannsdalstinden and the expanse of the Norwegian Sea begins only a few metres away. The higher you climb the more spectacular your surroundings become. Bounded by water and rock you are afforded a view from the summit across the archipelago. Nowhere on the Lofoten are you ever nearer to the sea and higher in the sky at the same time. A mountain of superlatives.

Right: blossoming Swedish dwarf cornel.
Below: ascent to Hermannsdalstinden.

Starting point: Forsfjorden, ferry dock, 3m. Reachable from Reine with the fjord ferry, 'MS Fjordskyss'. In Reine, drive to the Reinebringen walkers' car park, where the ferry dock is situated (timetable: reinefjorden.no or at the ferry dock and on the board outside the Co-op food shop). 2–3 departures daily from Reine (ca. 150 NOK). Make your stop really clear as Forsfjorden is not a regular destination.

End point: car park at the viewpoint on the E 10 south of Reine. Either hitchhike back to Reine, walk (2km) or cycle if you left a bike here beforehand for the purpose.

Grade: strenuous walk with some very steep sections, alpine terrain with easy climbing in the summit area, waymarked with cairns and red paint marks. Absolute surefootedness and a good head for heights are a must. Snowfields are still possible here into summer. The ascent via Forsfjorden is to be avoided after heavy rainfall.

Infrastructure: accommodation, cafés and restaurants in Reine, Sakrisøy and Hamnøy. Supermarket and petrol station in Reine. The unstaffed Munkebu hut is only available to members of the DNT (lofoten.dnt.no).

Alternative: it is also possible to start your ascent from Djupfjorden or Sørvågen. However, these ascents are longer.

Remarks: since the fjord boat leaves early in the afternoon, the descent to Forsfjorden is not an option. A pick-up should therefore be arranged before your walk (poor mobile phone coverage in the walking area). Please note: Hermannsdalstinden is inside the Lofotodden nasjonalpark where mountain biking and flying drones is not allowed.

Map: Vest-Lofoten.

At the ferry dock in **Forsfjorden** ❶ turn right around the turbine house of the hydroelectric plant. This is fed by water from all the lakes that you will pass on this walk. A red paint mark indicates the way up the extremely steep and very wet slope (to be avoided after heavy rainfall!). A power line and downpipe of the power plant accompany you at the start. You can easily lose your way here so be sure to look carefully for the few waymarkers. After a sweaty 40 minute ascent you reach Tennesvatnet lake and the path continues to climb to **P. 448** ❷ with good views over the large kidney-shaped Lake Krokvatnet.

The path to the south leads via the Lamheia to the Munkebu hut (your return path later on).

To reach Hermannsdalstinden, however, continue in a westerly direction. Descend 90 vertical metres and on the following steep slope go up onto the rocky bar located between the two lakes of Litlforsvatnet (on the right) and Krokvatnet (on the left). Finally, after some airy sections (narrow ridge with a rope for protection), you reach a large **plateau** ❸ covered in stones.

Continue along a narrow ridge to an altitude of 800m where you are now standing in front of the large scree slope below the summit. The elongated snowfield which is often in evidence until July, lends itself to a direct ascent. The waymarked path on the left leads across the scree slope. At an altitude of 970m, below the crag-like summit structure, the trace of a path runs westwards which then leads from the

View across to the Hermannsdalstinden.

south onto the summit with some easy climbing up through the boulders. On the easier and 'official' alternative you orientate yourself towards the gap that can be seen to the right of the summit. In this gully, often filled with snow for a long time, ascend first to the summit ridge and then to the west onto the airy summit of **Hermannsdalstinden** ❹.

Return back down to **P. 448** ❷ on the same path. From here ascend southwards to the narrow ridge that separates Krokvatnet and Tennesvatnet lakes. Ascend the opposite side and continue eastwards along the path to the hill where the **Munkebu** ❺ is located. From here walk for 10 minutes along the path heading south. Between Djupfjordheia, 510m, lying ahead of you and the huge massif of Munkan, 775m, in the east, a valley drops down to the Djupfjorden.

Look for the faintly visible path that runs eastwards here (very few cairns) and descend 475 vertical metres down to the **Djupfjorden** ❻. Some remains of walls can be seen between the tall grasses reminding you of the former settlement in this area. The Djupfjord bridge which you could see during the whole of your descent at the exit from the fjord, marks the end of your walk. Walk on the right hand side of the fjord across the former pastures belonging to the settlement. The terrain becomes increasingly overgrown with bushes and the route finding can be difficult. It's a tiresome slog across a wet, wooded hillside with boulders to the car park at the viewpoint on the **E 10** ❼. You can reach Reine either by hitchhiking or by bike which you left there beforehand.

↗ 220m | ↘ 220m | 7.2km
2.20 hrs

6 Vindstad – Bunesstranda

Beach walk to the outside edge of Moskenesøya

According to the legend, there were two sisters living on one of the farms in Bunes. They were so jealous of each other that one of them was envious of the other's lover to such a degree that she poisoned the whole property with mercury. Since then, there has only been sand and yet more sand in the entire bay…
Anyway, Bunes is one of those settlements on the outside edge of the Lofoten which were abandoned in the second half of the 20th century but are now popular destinations for day-trippers.

Starting point: Vindstad, ferry dock, 2m, reachable from Reine with the Fjord ferry 'MS Fjordskyss'. In Reine, drive to the Reinebringen walkers' car park, where the ferry dock is situated (you can find the timetable at reinefjorden.no or on the board outside the Co-op food shop and at the ferry dock). There are daily 2–3 departures in the season from Reine (50 NOK).
Grade: easy walk.
Infrastructure: small summer café in Vindstad. Various accommodations, cafés and restaurants in Reine, Sakrisøy and Hamnøy. There's a supermarket and petrol station in Reine.
Alternative: ascent of Helvetestinden, 602m, 530 vertical metres, 'black walk'; exposed ridge in places, some climbing in the summit area): from Einangen col ❸ an unclear visible path runs eastwards across an area of meadows to the col between Kammen, 514m, and Brunakseltinden, 513m. From the col, continue along the ridge in a northwesterly direction. Follow the clearly visible path to the summit of Helvetestinden via Brunakseltinden from where you get a magnificent view. Return the same way to Einangen col ❸.
Remarks: The area is inside the Lofotodden nasjonalpark where mountain biking and flying drones is not allowed.
Map: Vest-Lofoten.

*Photo above: Bunes beach is enormous and is an inviting place for a lovely stroll.
Left below: on your way with the fjord ferry.*

From the ferry dock in **Vindstad** ❶ walk along the gravel roadway beside the fjord as far as the houses of **Bunesfjorden** ❷ and there turn off onto the signposted footpath (Bunes Beach) which brings you up in the direction of Einangen. On the left hand side you can take a shortcut to the old cemetery. Before you reach **Einangen col** ❸ the path turns into a surfaced cart track.

Once you arrive at the top, you will notice that the col is actually an isthmus. In front of you lies the Norwegian Sea and behind you the Bunesfjorden which leads to the Vestfjorden. From here the view opens out onto the 2.5km² white sandy beach of Bunesstranda. The immense western rock face of Helvetestinden towers up on your right hand side. Well-trodden, steep paths bring you down onto the beach and you now have to walk a good 700m to reach the water of the **Norwegian Sea** ❹. You might be tempted to take a refreshing dip in the cold sea or follow a detour to the west past the Buneset estate to Ausodden headland.
Return the same way to **Vindstad** ❶.

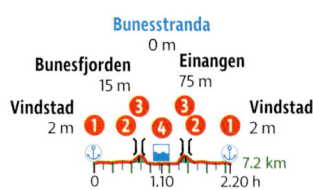

TOP 7

Reinebringen, 484m

↗ 505m | ↘ 505m | 6.0km
3.10 hrs

Breathtaking beauty on Moskenesøya

Reinebringen towers over the fishing village of Reine on the E 10 on Moskenesøya. Inspite of its modest height it affords the walker such a spectacular panorama that this mountain is a must for many visitors. However, in recent years this mountain has almost been 'loved to death'. In addition to the inherent difficulties and weather-related damage the increasing number of walkers have caused severe erosion damage. For this reason, Sherpas have built a continuous staircase of natural stones along the southern flank of the Reinebringen massif. However, the staircase only eases the strenuous ascent insofar as they stop the damage to the ground; the ascent is still exhausting and hard on your joints.

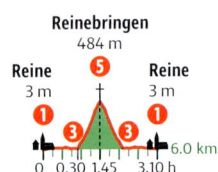

View from Reinbringen of Reine and the surrounding area.

Starting point: Reine (Ytre Hamn), signposted paid walkers' car park at the outermost port, 3 m.
Infrastructure: accommodation, cafés and restaurants in Reine, Sakrisøy and Hamnøy. Supermarket and petrol station in Reine.
Grade: signposted footpath, partially with natural stone stairs. Extremely steep ascents; 400m of altitude over 1.1km.
Tips: in Reine and Sakrisøy various activities can be booked: fishing, paddle boat tours (the hiring of sea kayaks is only possible with a våtkart, equivalent to EPP2 respectively BCU 2Star; see p. 31), boat trips, walks to the Lofotodden and to the Kollhellaren cave (also called Revsvikhula), where you can gaze in wonder at the rock paintings. Bikes can be hired too.
At the information centre of the Lofotodden nasjonalpark which is inside the building of the Galleri Eva Harr you can visit a small exhibition which is worth seeing.
Museums: Å – Norwegian Fishing Village Museum and Lofoten Stockfish Museum; Sørvågen – Norwegian Telecommunications Museum; Sakrisøy – Lofoten Toy Museum; Sund – Sund Fisheries Museum with a forge.
Remarks: 1. Reinebringen is one of the most accident-prone mountains in Norway. The area around the summit ridge frequently sees accidents, which can be fatal. The ascent itself is not particularly difficult due to the Sherpa stairs, however, the steepness should not be underestimated. Please observe the warning signs at the start of the mountain path. In wet weather, strong winds and during the months of November to April, it is not advisable to climb the stairs.
2. The small town of Reine is a must-see of the Lofoten, which also means that it is crowded with tourists, especially in summer. There are not enough parking spaces in the village. Please use the indicated car park at the port (there is also fresh water and toilets), motorhomes are allowed to park here overnight. Here is also the ferry dock for the fjord boat to Vinstad (see Walks 5 and 6).
Map: Vest-Lofoten.

The tour starts at the walkers' car park at the outermost port (Ytre Hamn) in **Reine** ❶. A road takes you to the village centre where you find a petrol station, cafés, restaurants and rorbuer. Follow the main road to the left, past the Eva Harr Galleri and the Lofotodden National Park Centre until you reach the **Reinehalsen viewpoint** ❷ at the junction with the E 10. From here, you can enjoy one of the famous views of the picturesque village. Behind the crash barrier, follow the E10 along the footpath towards Å. Just before you reach the entrance of the Ramsvik tunnel, the road of the old E 10 leads you around the Reinebringen massif.

The rorbuer in Reine make a lovely photo – a famous motif.

On the other side of the tunnel near the exit, you **start** your **ascent** ❸ of the southern flank of the mountain with a rest area made of natural stones and information boards. From here, climb the 1978 steps that lead up to the ridge of Reinebringen. On the first few metres, you cross a birch forest, walk under a power line and reach a little bridge, where a small stream drops down into a small waterfall. The path continues through the birch forest, and after 100 vertical metres you get a clear view of Ramsvika bay below you and the Vestfjorden. On the way, there are several stone benches to rest, which are probably there because of the extreme steepness of the climb. The birch forest thins out, and you reach the dwarf shrub zone. Below the rocky foothills of the eastern summit, the stairway swings to the left into a gully that leads up a good 100 vertical metres to a **col** ❹. Those who know what erosion looks like will recognise the damage the old path has done on the way up. From the col, you get a breathtaking view down to Reine, the Reinefjorden and the surrounding mountains. To the right, over two rocky ledges, a short climb would take you to the eastern viewpoint of Reinebringen, 449m. However, you follow the steps to the left and take the well-trodden path across a meadow slope which takes you to a small summit plateau on the ridge of **Reinebringen** ❺, 484m.
Return to the starting point of the walk in **Reine** ❶ along the same path. Do not underestimate the descent – the stairs can be tiring.

↗ 360m | ↘ 360m | 4.3km
2.00 hrs

Solbjørnvatnet and Tekoppstetten, 365m 8

Onto Moskenesøya's northeastern peak

It's a short walk to Solbjørnvatnet lake and to Tekoppstetten and not all that difficult. Inspite of its modest height you quickly find yourself in seemingly alpine territory with beautiful views into the mountains on the northeastern side of Moskenesøya.

Starting point: Mølnarodden, car park behind the parish hall, diagonally opposite the salmon farm, 15m. Coming from Reine along the E 10 about 2.4km north of the Fjøsdalen tunnel or from Flakstadøya 1km south of Kåkernbrua bridge.
Grade: moderate walk, unmarked, occasional cairns, difficult route finding at times, boggy in places, some easy climbing in the summit area. Attention: the rocky sections can be very slippery when wet.
Infrastructure: accommodation, cafés and restaurants in Reine, Sakrisøy and Hamnøy. Supermarket and petrol station in Reine.
Tip: In Sund there's the small Sund Fisheries Museum with a forge and exhibition of boat engines. Here you can see where the steel cormorants are made that you see in many places.
Map: Vest-Lofoten.

Solbjørnvatnet.

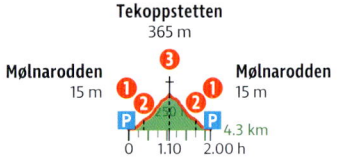

A gravel roadway starts from behind the parish hall of **Mølnarodden ❶** which has a barrier across it. Follow this path for a good 300m until you come to a stony path on the right which leads over a little stream. The following path now leads you across meadows and boggy terrain up onto a horizontal bar of rock which you can see up ahead and which you will have to climb. On the way, the path turns right and to the north and is occasionally waymarked with cairns. Once you have climbed over the **ledge of rock ❷** you will see small lakes lying between rocks polished smooth by glaciers, and areas of peat. As you wander about here you can look down on the large Solbjørnvatnet lake and gaze at the surrounding mountain landscape. Continue northwards as far as the slopes of the Tekoppstetten massif which rises up ahead and look

On the way up to Tekoppstetten.

for a path that brings you up and round to the left. The route finding is a bit tricky and several times you are walking across areas of bare rock. From here you can enjoy an airy, but fabulous panorama of the Solbjørnvatnet and the surrounding landscape.
Before the last ascent cross over a sloping rocky plateau. The summit is reached by making an easy climb from the right hand side. From the top of **Tekoppstetten** ❸ which is not all that high, you have an amazing view across the alpine landscape of northeastern Moskenesøya as well as northwards across the Kåkersundet and the southern foothills of the island of Flakstadøya opposite.
Return the same way to the **starting point** ❶.

9 Kvalvika

TOP

↗ 360m | ↘ 360m | 7.0km
3.00 hrs

Sunbathing at whale bay

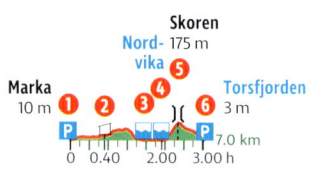

The walk to Kvalvika is one of the most famous walks on the Lofoten. You should take a whole day over the route described below as the many secluded places, the sandy beaches and the beautiful and atmospheric environment allows you to leave all your cares behind. Most visitors take the shortest route directly from the Torsfjorden across the Skoren col. At the time of the midnight sun the beaches of Kvalvika are overrun when everyone is making their pilgrimage to the beach with children and picnic equipment.

Kvalvika bay with a view of Fuglhuken and Ryten.

Starting point: Marka, 10m. On the E 10 south of Ramberg turn off to Fredvang, drive across two arch bridges, follow the signs left to Fredvang-Sentrum and drive about 3.2km along the road beside the Torsfjorden – this is where the walk ends (or starts for the shorter version). Continue following the road and turn right at a T-junction, drive along the gravel road beside the Selfjorden and after about 1.3km in Marka there's a parking bay on the left hand side.
End point: Torsfjorden, 3m, see above. In order to save yourself the 4km long walk back along the road to the starting point, it's a good idea to leave a bike there beforehand.
Grade: well-trodden, clear path with boggy areas as well as sections of rock and scree, the Kuhella rocky ledge (protected with a chain) can prove to be a bit difficult.
Infrastructure: campsite, rorbuer and B&B in Fredvang and also Ramberg. Restaurant, café, supermarket and petrol station in Ramberg.
Alternative: the most popular route to Kvalvika is the route from Kvalvika to Torsfjorden, described as the return route in this walk (there and back 2 hrs, 340 vertical metres, signposted at the parking bay on the Torsfjorden). Attention: There is a central car park at the old school in Fredvang. A bus shuttle to Torsfjorden operates during the summer months.
Linking tip: from Kvalvika you can make an ascent of Ryten, 543m (Walk 10).
Remarks: The bay of Kvalvika is inside the Lofotodden nasjonalpark where mountain biking and flying drones is not allowed.
Map: Vest-Lofoten.

From the car park in **Marka** ❶ start your walk by heading northwards along a clear path that leads over wooden footbridges across a large boggy area as far as a small col. Markvatnet lake now lies ahead and you descend to its eastern side where you pass a large birchwood. The stony path in dry weather turns into a muddy track after heavy rainfall. At the end of the Markvatnet you come to a simple **shepherds' hut** ❷. You will find some information about the old settlement once located here in the 'hut book'. Now ascend slowly in a northwesterly direction up across meadows flanked by the high, anthracite-coloured rock faces of Litljordtindan, 751m.

Ågotvatnet lake lies wedged in below the rock massif. The path on the eastern side of the lake leads across some very stony terrain and towards the end ascends to a col. The rock faces open out at the top to give you an open view down to the Norwegian Sea and the western part of Kvalvika bay. To the north you can see the rock faces of Ryten, 543m, and Fuglhuken, 557m, steeply rising out of the sea.

Walk down the slope, past Kvalvikvatnet lake, over high sand dunes and down to **Vestervika beach** ❸. In order to reach the second part of Kvalvika, the sandy beach of Nordvika, you have to overcome the rocky promontory

Crossing the boggy area at Markvatnet lake.

of Kuhella (meaning 'cow's hell'). A chain-secured path leads over the sloping rock slabs and another chain helps you down a 2.5m high rock ledge. Younger children and people who are not used to climbing will need a bit of help here. As an alternative you could follow the sheep paths which cross the steep meadow slope above. When the water is really low it is possible to walk directly over the sandy beach.

After this section of the walk the path continues further on along the edge of the sloping meadow around **Nordvika** beach. However, instead, scramble directly down over some boulders to the round 500m wide **beach** ❹. Further along the huge beach area, you will find fire pits, benches and shelters made out of drift wood. A fresh water stream runs along the northern side. The whole ambiance of the place lends itself to a lengthy break.

For your return take the path that leads out of the bay southeastwards across Skoren col. Looking back on your way across the meadowland you are aware of the foundation walls of the former small settlement of Kvalvika lying hidden under the grass. The path becomes increasingly stony and several tracks appear. Once you reach the top of **Skoren** ❺ you can see Torsfjorden and Selfjorden. Walk across an extensive boggy area (boardwalks) down to the **Torsfjorden** ❻. The walk ends here.

In order to return to your starting point you have to turn right at the road and walk another 4km back to **Marka** ❶ or cycle back having left a bike there beforehand.

Billion year old massifs are reflected in Ågotvatnet lake.

↗ 890m | ↘ 890m | 10.0km
4.20 hrs

10 Ryten, 543m

Walk over Ryten to Kvalvika

Ryten and its 14m higher brother Fuglhuken tower up like a huge cliff on the north side of Kvalvika, the whale bay, out of the sea. It's an intoxicating view as you ascend to the summit and well worth the effort, but take special care not to harm the environment as you make your way up. The walk can easily be combined with Walk 9 (Kvalvika) or undertaken as a detour from it.

Starting point: Indresand, signposted paid car park, 2m. 1.5km northwest of Fredvang on the road to Indresand and Ytresand.
Grade: waymarked, clearly visible and frequently walked path, at times boggy and with some steep sections, boardwalks.
Infrastructure: campsite, accommodation in Fredvang and Ramberg. Restaurant, café, supermarket and petrol station in Ramberg.

Linking tip: you can combine your return route with Walk 9.
Remarks: Kvalvika and Ryten are inside the Lofotodden nasjonalpark where mountain biking and flying drones is not allowed.
Tips: Fredvang with its surrounding areas is the starting point for Walks 9, 10 and 12. There are two pretty sandy beaches, a small turf museum and two bridges with an interesting architecture.
Map: Vest-Lofoten.

From the southern end of the car park in **Indresand** ❶, a path leads across meadows and continues on boardwalks over boggy terrain in an easterly direction. You come to a track that you follow to the end of the valley and there it turns into a stony path which leads up to a small col with a lake. Turn west, continue uphill and on the right hand side as you walk along, you can enjoy a panorama over the bay of Sandbotn. At an altitude of 200m cross a boggy area. The path you have been following up to now heads northwestwards around a hill, but take the path instead that leads

The two beaches of Kvalvika attract many visitors.

steeply up to the **Fredvanghytta** ❷ on the east side of this hill, from where you can enjoy a magnificent view. Continue now in a westerly direction across a boggy depression (boardwalks) on a flat **col** ❸ above Forsvatnet lake (large cairn). In front of us lies the wide grassy ridge of Ryten. The path climbs gently up to the western edge of the Ryten massif from where you have a first view of the bay of Kvalvika, 350m below. The path ascends up along the edge of the mountain to the summit plateau of **Ryten** ❹, at the end of which a stone tower marks the highest point.

Return down the same path to the **col** ❸. In order to reach Kvalvika, continue past the north side of Forsvatnet lake. The path leads across boardwalks that have been put up to protect the boggy meadows. Follow a steep descent parallel to the course of a stream into the bay of **Kvalvika** ❺. The **way back** leads across the **col** ❸ and the **Fredvanghytta** ❷ to **Indresand** ❶.

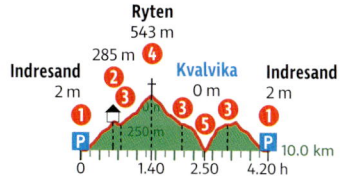

↗ 60m | ↘ 60m | 3.6km
1.20 hrs

11 Mulstøa

A short walk along the coast

A beautiful, gentle family walk along an old coastal path to the abandoned settlement of Mulstøa. You can watch the sunsets and the midnight sun from here on the outer edge of Moskenesøya and have a truly magical day.

Starting point: Ytresand, small car park, 15m. On the E 10 south of Ramberg follow the signs to Fredvang and Ytresand. There is an alternative parking in Indresand (1.2km).
Grade: unmarked, easy coastal walk, some boggy sections and some sections covered in scree.
Infrastructure: campsite, accommodation in Fredvang and Ramberg. Restaurant, café, supermarket and petrol station in Ramberg.
Tips: the starting point for Walks 9, 10 and 12 is Fredvang and surrounding area. There are two beautiful sandy beaches, a small peat museum and two architecturally interesting bridges.
Map: Vest-Lofoten.

On the way to Mulstøa.

View of Sandbotnen, Ytresand and the Flakstad chain of mountains.

Start your walk from the car park at the end of the surfaced road in **Ytresand** ❶ where a signpost indicates the way to Mulstøa. Climb over the pasture fence and follow the signpost on the left across the hillside. The walk runs along the shallow Sandbotnen bay with its wide sandy beach and the gleaming blue sea. Offshore lies the small island of Sandøya where sheep graze in summer. Looking eastwards you can see the mountain ranges of Flakstadøya. To your left rises up the mountain ridge which you walk along to Litlberget (see Walk 12).

The quality of the path varies greatly along the route and sometimes you have to overcome some rocky sections with scree. The old road that once led to Mulstøa can still be seen in places. After prolonged or heavy rain there are short muddy sections and slippery scree. After a good kilometre you reach a promontory. You can watch the breakers from here and look across the skerries of Fredvang. Continue further along and walk round a bend in the path over a rocky notch – Hundsslåka.

Just a small incline still to climb before you descend into the bay of **Mulstøa** ❷. You are greeted by a **meadow area** strewn with rocks with a visitors' book and some private property with a fence around it, a small sandy beach, the wide open Norwegian Sea and the bay with its offshore skerries. **Return** the same way.

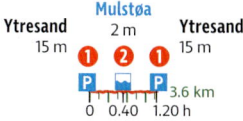

12 Litlberget, 281m

↗ 390m | ↘ 390m | 5.5km
2.00 hrs

Above the abandoned settlements of Mulstøa and Stokkvika

The walk to Litlberget and the possible continuation as far as Stokkvika is a lovely walk and not too strenuous. From Litlberget you see Mulstøa and its offshore skerries and trace the course of the midnight sun. The beach of Stokkvika is remote and wild and so is the elongated Stokkvikdalen with Stokkvikelva stream draining down from the hillsides. No sheep have been grazing here for a long time and so the dense, tall grasses create sweeping hilly landscapes.

Starting point: Ytresand, small car park, 15m. On the E 10 south of Ramberg follow the signs to Fredvang and Ytresand. Alternative parking in Indresand (1.2km, see Walk 10).
Grade: clear path which is waymarked at times, with a somewhat steeper incline onto the heia. You must be very careful if there's fog or low cloud as you can very easily lose your way on the heia.

Infrastructure: campsite, accommodation in Fredvang as well as Ramberg. Restaurant, café, supermarket and petrol station in Ramberg.
Alternative: descent to Stokkvika bay (various paths) where you can still see the remains of the former settlement. There's a small shelter available. The exact description can be found on the opposite page.
Map: Vest-Lofoten.

Start your walk from the car park at the end of the surfaced road in **Ytresand** ❶. Immediately after climbing over the sheep fence a sign indicates left to the path to Stokkvika. Ascend southwestwards up the mountain slope and on your left hand side you will see a small mountain lake in a valley basin (drinking water supply for local use). Your path turns to the north and winds its way steeply uphill to **Ytresandheia** plateau. Now orientate yourself along the path that runs relatively close to the edge of the mountain ridge. On the right hand side you look down into Sandbotnen bay and across to the moun-

Stokkvika's old pastureland.

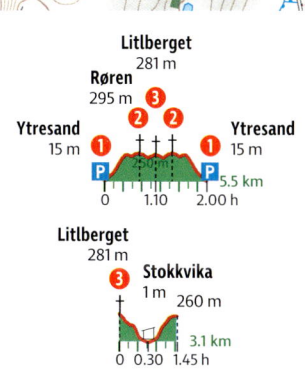

tain chain of Flakstadøya. On the left hand side you can clearly see the traces of former peat digging. Then follows a short intermediary descent across a depression and after that the path heads for the summit of the next rise, **Røren** ❷. Walk for about 250m still keeping to the edge of the mountain ridge before you take the well-trodden path that brings you round a northwestern bend onto the clearly visible summit of **Litlberget** ❸. The Norwegian Sea spreads out in front of you. Take the same path to return to your **starting point** ❶.

Alternative: those keen for adventure can extend the walk with a detour to the former settlement of Stokkvika (from Litlberget 1.45 hrs, 280m ascent, 300m descent, a 'red walk'; meadow paths but somewhat unclear at times, route finding skills necessary).

From the summit of **Litlberget** ❸ follow a well-trodden path that descends to the west. With a bird's eye view you can see the old drainage ditches and field boundaries of the former settlement. The path leads in an arc onto the southwest flank of the mountain to a small boggy area. The source of a stream that flows down to Stokkvika is located here. Descend on the left hand side of the stream down to the meadowland. The narrow path now descends over meadows, swamps and streams to the arc-shaped pebbly beach which is exposed to the full force of the Norwegian Sea. A small refuge provides shelter in stormy winds. On your return go back up beside the stream to the boggy area. From here there's no need to take the path back to Litlberget and Røren, continue instead up along the right hand side of the valley; there's a long drawn out boggy area on your left. Cross over this boggy area at the end in a southeasterly direction (route finding quite tricky) and walk along a path as far as the small depression between Røren and Ytresandheia where you meet up with your outward path.

↗ 500m | ↘ 500m | 5.3km

13 Volandstinden, 457m

2.30 hrs 🚍

Between tidal currents and fjords

The Volandstinden is a distinctive, cone-shaped mountain that rises up at the northern end of the left hand Flakstad 'rib'. Like a watchman, it sits enthroned above the Torsfjorden, the Røssøystraumen tidal stream and the Skjelfjorden. From April to May 1940, a number of British and Allied ships were able to find refuge in the Skjelfjorden before being discovered by the German troops. In 1944 the Germans established POW camps here and the prisoners of war (most of them were Russian) had to build bunkers. Some of these bunkers still exist today and you are able to visit them and have a look around.

Starting point: Skjelfjord, first house on the right, 26m. From Ramberg travel south on the E 10 to the Skjelfjord turn-off, turn left here onto the Fv 7592, then turn right after 900m; park here.
Grade: clearly visible, good walkable path, but steep and exposed in the summit area.
Infrastructure: campsite, accommodation, restaurant, café, supermarket and petrol station in Ramberg. Friisgarden, in the oldest house of Ramberg, cosy café and restaurant.
Tip: If you drive about 500m back in the direction of the E 10 you come to a tower, the 'Epitaph' by Toshikatsu Endo (Skulpturlandskap project of Nordland). 50m further on you can take a stroll through a well-hidden WWII German bunker complex.
Map: Vest-Lofoten.

Behind the lone-standing, light brown house in **Skjelfjord** ❶ you will find the start of a path leading southwestwards across soggy meadows towards the mountain slope. After 15 minutes a valley widens out on the right and you cross a stream and pass a shelter (gapahuk). Now go directly under the power line steeply up the slope. After ne-

*Photo above: curved bridge constructions connect Flakstadøya with Moskenesøya.
Left: the prominent peak of Volandstinden rises into the sky.*

gotiating two rocky steps, the path swings to the left up a heath-covered slope that leads to a hill ❷ with a cairn. Cross the stream a bit lower down and the marshy slope on the opposite side before you reach a broad saddle. From here, climb over the broad ridge northwards towards the summit. Shortly before the summit ridge you cross a small scree slope (indistinct traces of a path) and walk on the western side of the mountain below the ridge to the summit of **Volandstinden** ❸ which is waymarked with a stone tower.

For those of you who do not suffer from vertigo, make the short detour onto the northern **pre-summit** ❹ which offers a magnificent view of the many islands below you.

Return along the same path back to the **starting point** ❶.

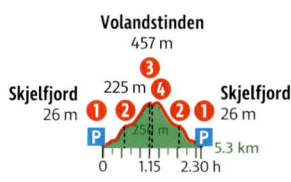

14 Flakstadtinden, 484m

↗ 480m | ↘ 480m | 4.3km
2.30 hrs

Above the beaches of Flakstadøya

Jørgine ('Gina') Anna Sverdrup Krog, known as Gina Krog, daughter of a parish priest and born in Flakstad in 1847, was one of the most uncompromising women's rights activists in Europe. From 1880 onwards and throughout her lifetime she demanded full equality for men and women. Thanks to her commitment Norway was the fourth country to introduce universal voting rights for women in 1913. Queen Sonja of Norway inaugurated the Ginaløypa footpath in Flakstad for the centenary. This is the path you will follow on the first part of your walk to Gapahuk.

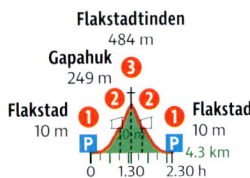

Grade: the initially easy walk has some especially steep sections in the second half and is exposed in the summit area. Clearly defined path with waymarkers and signposts.
Infrastructure: campsite, accommodation, restaurant, café, supermarket and petrol station in Ramberg. Campsite on Skagen beach.
Starting point: Flakstad, car park at the cemetery, 10m, alternative parking at the church. From the supermarket in Ramberg drive 3.7km northeastwards along the E 10. At the signpost, turn into the direction of Flakstad and Skagen campsite.
Tips: the church in Flakstad is worth a visit. The buildings belonging to the old vicarage (private property) are located just next to it. On Skagen beach you are able to hire surfing, SUP and kayak gear as well as book courses.
Map: Vest-Lofoten.

View of Hustinden (691m) across the Vareidsundet.

Flakstad church.

From the car park in **Flakstad** ❶ walk back to the E 10 and turn left here in the direction of Leknes. After 400m you come to a large electricity pylon and the actual start of the footpath. Walk under the power line to the south where you orientate yourself towards the valley lying ahead with Middagselva stream.

The well-trodden path which is covered in scree in many places, runs uphill across the right hand slope of the valley. At a height of 240m, a good 1km after the start of the actual footpath (at the large electricity pylon on the road), you reach **Gapahuk** ❷, the shelter that marks the end of the Ginaløypa path. Looking southwestwards you can see the prominent peak of Stortinden, 866m, with its dramatically steep rock face.

From this point you have to climb 240 vertical metres steeply uphill. Ascend the southeastern flank of Flakstadtinden. You reach the ridge a short distance below your destination and change over onto the northern side of the mountain. The last few metres go left up through some boulders to the 484m high summit of **Flakstadtinden** ❸. You look down from here onto the wonderful white beaches of Flakstad and its picturesque church. Hustinden, 691m, rises up opposite you in the north.

The **descent** follows the same route.

15 From Nesland to Nusfjord

↗ 490m | ↘ 490m | 9.8km
4.00 hrs

TOP

A varied walk for everyone

Nesland and Nusfjord villages situated on the Vestfjorden are of very different character and each has its own charm. Vester and Auster Nesland are two small charming fishing villages which lie on a ruggedly picturesque stretch of coast which lends itself to closer investigation. Nusfjord used to be a fishing village and also an important trading post. Today it is a large museum village with café, country store, fish oil distillery, blacksmith, port and rorbuer complex. The largely preserved historic buildings with colourful wooden houses and rorbuer, and its location in the narrow fjord flanked by high mountains, make up the charm of Nusfjord. Although it is stated again and again – Nusfjord is not on the UNESCO World Heritage List.

Worthwhile: taking a break or going for something to eat in picturesque Nusfjord.

Starting point: Auster Nesland, car park at the end of the gravel road, 2m. 2km south of Flakstad turn off the E 10 to Skjelfjord and follow the road for 10km (6km of gravel surface).
Grade: waymarked, very clear path, varied and easily walkable coastal path, in places across the sloping hillside; places secured with a chain and a ladder where needed, section of boulders and boggy areas.
Infrastructure: rorbuer, café and restaurant in Nusfjord; supermarket and petrol station in Ramberg.
Alternative: the walk can also be started in Nusfjord. In this case follow the gravel road from the centre of Nusfjord in a southerly direction until it turns into an old roadway. The footpath then turns off to the right here (sign for Fiskersti).
Linking tip: this walk can be extended by continuing along the footpath from Kilan to Napp (Alternative of Walk 17) or Tønsåsheia (Walk 16).
Remark: the Lofoten mountain range protects the path along the coast from the wind and rain. The sun frequently shines here while, on the outer side of Flakstadøya, the weather is often unpleasant.
Map: Vest-Lofoten.

Auster Nesland is a small old fishing village which was permanently inhabited until the 1970s. Especially in winter, it was often cut off from the outside world by storms and avalanches. The footpath to Nusfjord begins behind the last old houses of **Auster Nesland** ❶. An information board explains the significance of this old fishermen's path.
The path brings you quickly over some rocky sections at about 40m above sea level and a view looking back reveals a beautiful view over Nesland and towards the island of Moskenesøya. It continues comfortably at the same

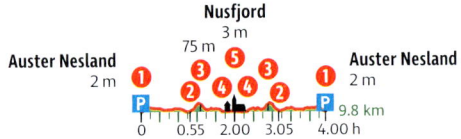

height, past a hill with a collection of cairns and a signal for navigation. Vedvika bay is located shortly afterwards on the right hand side and a path leads down to it. Take the path around the bay and above it by walking through a small birchwood and across boggy terrain in places. Walk across a bridge over a small mountain stream.

The next section gets a bit rockier and in one place is protected with chains. Shortly afterwards you come to a **rockfall ❷**. You have to scramble in a leftward curve over the boulders. You can often observe seals in the small bay below the rockfall.

Sea kayak trip between Nesland and Nusfjord.

View of Vester Nesland and the Moskenesøya chain of mountains.

Continue across the very varied landscape until you see Lyrvika bay way down below. At this point you need to keep to the left and follow the sandy and well-trodden path up the hillside (otherwise, all of a sudden, you find yourself on the old footpath that is no longer in use). A little bit later on descend through a gap where there is a tallish **ladder** ❸ to help you. The final part of the path leads you downhill to a stream and after you have crossed it, continue across an undulating area of land where there are some boggy sections. Finally you are standing at a rocky ledge where you keep to the right in order to descend to a **gravel track** ❹. This track leads you into the centre of **Nusfjord** ❺ where you can take a break with coffee, cake and an ice cream.

For the **way back** to **Auster Nesland** ❶ follow the same route.

16 Tønsåsheia, 769m

↗ 850m | ↘ 850m | 8.8km
4.30 hrs

Nusfjord vertical

Tønsåsheia belongs to the southern part of the mountain range which stretches from north to south along the central 'rib' of Flakstadøya. The peaks of the mountain chain reach up to 934m (Stjerntinden), rugged cliffs drop east and west to the fjords and lakes. The ascent of Tønsåsheia starts from the picturesque former trading and fishing village of Nusfjord, a wonderful place to while away some time after your walk.

High above Lyrvika bay.

Starting point: Nusfjord, car park, 20m. There's an entry fee for Nusfjord.
Grade: waymarked in places with cairns. The start of the climb is quite difficult to find since there are no waymarkers. Otherwise it's a steep, but easily negotiated and visible path, snowfields in the summit area can still last into June.
Infrastructure: rorbuer, café and restaurant, country store in Nusfjord. Supermarket and petrol station in Ramberg.
Tips: Nusfjord is an old trading and fishing village well worth a visit. If you start the walk early enough then you will still have time to eat in Nusfjord afterwards. Otherwise, take a leisurely stroll through the tiny, now empty streets and enjoy the evening atmosphere. Staying overnight in Nusfjord has a special charm due to the authenticity of the place and the rorbuer.
Map: Vest-Lofoten.

Start the walk from the car park in **Nusfjord** ❶ and follow the road leading to the historic village centre. Continue in a southerly direction past the port until the gravel road turns into an old roadway. Here, turn right for the hiking path (sign for Fiskersti). About 250m after leaving the gravel road and overcoming the first rock steps, quite a large depression follows at the end

of which an inconspicuous small **path ❷** branches off to the right. Continue through meadows with birch shrubs for about 100m in a northerly direction before the path turns to the west and you ascend higher and higher across a landscape of round, smooth rocky hillocks. You quickly gain height; far below lie Nusfjord and the Vestfjorden. The path leads you onto an elongated rocky ridge, 311m, which you walk round across a gravel slope on the left side (danger of slipping).

After that keep southwest across a varied terrain until you come to a large **hill ❸** with a fantastic view over the Vestfjorden. To the right your path now ascends 180 vertical metres steeply up the mountain hillside onto the summit plateau and then you walk across a gently sloping incline for another 10 minutes to reach the summit of **Tønsåsheia ❹**.

Walk back the same way to **Nusfjord ❶**.

On Tønsåsheia.

17 Napp – Andopen

↗ 190m | ↘ 190m | 7.2km
2.00 hrs

Along the Nappstraumen

A lovely and easy walk along beside the tidal waves of Nappstraumen which divides the islands of Flakstadøya and Vestvågøya. On Vestvågøya you are accompanied by Hornsheia and Haugheia and also the mountain chain with Skottinden as its highest peak. The extension of the walk leads to the Stone Age cave of Storbåthellaren and as far as Kilan.

Andopen lies in a charming location on the Nappstraumen, far away from any roads.

Starting point: Napp, port, 6m. In Napp take the road branching off to the port area from the E 10 and follow it to the end. Park on the gravel square.
Grade: easy coastal walk with boggy sections, T-waymarkers; quite difficult to find at the start.
Infrastructure: accommodation and restaurants in Leknes, Nusfjord and Ramberg; supermarkets and petrol stations in Leknes and Ramberg.
Alternative: continuation of the walk to Kilan; see the opposite page.
Map: Vest-Lofoten.

The coastal path to Andopen begins on the southern side of the gravel square at the port in **Napp** ❶ behind a sheep fence and a ditch. Orientate yourself by following the power line which runs relatively close to the path. The waymarking at the start is rather poor and can be frustrating. There are several paths running along at different heights, all of which merge at a point that is secured with a ladder and chain (this can be bypassed below). After 20 minutes you pass the old **Hårberget** estate where the path leads up round the back of it. From here there are cairns and red T-waymarkers. After another 30 minutes on a grassy hill you find a recently restored Nordland house (the path seems to lead directly to it). The path runs around the eastern side of this property in an arc and after another 10 minutes you reach the scattered remains of stables and houses belonging to the old settlement of **Andopen** ❷. The preserved buildings are still used as holiday homes today. A dammed lake and a shallow bay invite you to linger for a while.
Return the same way to **Napp** ❶.

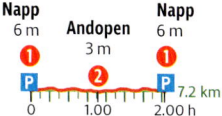 

Alternative: extend the walk as far as **Kilan** (3.30 hrs from Andopen, 9.3km, 570 vertical metres, a 'red' walk, cairns and T-waymarkers).

The bay of **Andopsvika** can be crossed at low tide, alternatively there's a path running along beside the western rock face. 10 minutes later you pass the outflow from Sørdalsvatnet lake (bridge). Here you can observe the change between the outflowing water from the lake and the rising tidal waves. You come to a rock barrier shortly afterwards where you ascend a steep gully (about 100 vertical metres where you will need the use of your hands) onto a glacial plateau. From here descend steeply down to the turn-off to the **Storbåthellaren** cave, the oldest known Stone Age dwelling place on the Lofoten.

The path continues in a southerly direction at an average altitude of 40 to 80m to a small col where you change over from the Nappstraumen to Flakstadpollen. The path now runs northwestwards, past the lakes of Straumøyvatnet and Ølkonvatnet, onto a small hill. A short descent and the crossing of a boggy pasture bring you to the car park for walkers on the E 10 that lies at the southern end of the hamlet of Kilan on the Flakstadpollen.

18 Stornappstinden, 740m

↗ 675m | ↘ 675m | 4.7km
3.30 hrs

Forebidding and indomitable…

…is how the massif appears with the Stornappstinden and Ramntinden peaks, at least when viewed from Offersøykammen (Walk 22). Once you reach the starting point, Nappskaret, the area widens out and a path leading uphill now becomes apparent. The summit of Stornappstinden affords views of the Stjerntinden chain of mountains in the central area of Flakstadøya and towards Moskenesøya. Nevertheless, the most breathtaking panorama is in the direction of Offersøykammen and right across Vestvågøya all the way to Austvågøya.

Starting point: car park at the vannverk (waterworks) just below Nappskaret col at the E 10, 60m. Shortly after (coming from Leknes) or shortly before (coming from Ramberg) the col, turn off right or left to the small waterworks. The car park is located after 120m on the left hand side.
Grade: unmarked path, very steep in places.
Infrastructure: accommodation and restaurants in Leknes, Nusfjord and Ramberg; supermarkets and petrol stations in Leknes and Ramberg.
Tip: if you turn north off the E 10 in Vareid, you will come to the Glashytta (glass blowing workshop) in Vikten where you can watch the glass blowing and have something to eat or drink in the small café.
Map: Vest-Lofoten.

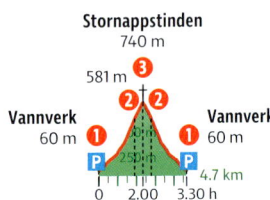

Photo above: the view from Stornappstinden across the whole of Vestvågøya (Offersøykammen in the foreground, Himmeltindan massif on the left) as far as Vågakallen (on the right beyond). – Left: on Nappskaret col.

From the car park **vannverk (waterworks)** ❶ continue along the roadway to a ski lift. Turn to the right here and walk parallel to the lift complex as far as the upper end. From here, at the western hillside of Litlnappstinden, 354m, turn northwards into a small valley where there's a stretch of boggy ground. The path continues in a northeasterly direction steeply up the hillside, in places round hairpin bends and over rough ground. In quite a few areas the sheep tracks running across the slope can easily be mistaken for the path. At an altitude of 580m you reach the broad **summit ridge** ❷ from where you are rewarded with a fantastic view towards the Norwegian Sea. From here continue your way across the gently sloping mountainside to the top of **Stornappstinden** ❸. Return the same way to the **vannverk** ❶.

↗ 740m | ↘ 740m | 6.2km
3.30 hrs

19 Skottinden, 671m

The Matterhorn of the Lofoten

Skottinden rises up to a point from the mountain ridge which runs from north to south along the Nappstraumen at the furthest southwestern point of Vestvågøya island. It is recognisable from a long way off on account of its striking silhouette. Skottinden is a real challenge. The ascent is steep and there are some climbing sections to be overcome in the summit area.

Starting point: car park for walkers (info board) on the road to Vetting, 3m. Drive south from Leknes on the Fv 818 to Gravdal, turn right there following the signs to Gravdal Sentrum/Nordlandssykehuset. After 130m, turn right and after 280m turn left onto the Sundsveien (Fv 7618). 1.8km later the tarmac road ends. Continue roughly another 2km southwards on the gravel road along Nappstraumen as far as the car park. Private road from here onwards.
Grade: few waymarkers, in the lower meadow area sometimes unclear path, in several sections extremely steep, exposed path, excellent surefootedness and a lack of vertigo are required, some easy climbing in the summit area. In no way attempt when wet! Risk of falling!
Infrastructure: accommodation, restaurants, cafés, supermarkets, petrol stations in Leknes.
Map: Vestvågøy.

From the **car park for walkers ❶** between Sund and Vetting walk a good kilometre along the private gravel road. Shortly before the last farmstead in **Vetting ❷** a sign on the left hand side marks the start of a meadow path that runs in the direction of Vittingstinden, 369m. Walk up through a steep gully on

The prominent peak of Skottinden.

On the summit of Skottinden.

the northern flank of the mountain and after that cross the hillside by ascending onto a small **col** ❸. A large hill criss-crossed by a myriad of sheep tracks now lies ahead. You can see Skottinden to the east and you walk towards its flank where the narrow, increasingly steep path continues uphill on its southwestern side. You need to overcome a few sections of easy climbing in the area around the summit strewn with boulders. A memorial below the summit is a reminder of a tragic fall that occurred in 1995.

From the top of **Skottinden** ❹ you are afforded a fabulous panorama across the Vestfjorden, the neighbouring island of Flakstadøya and also the whole of Vestvågøya. An impressive landsscape of lakes and islands lies way down below.

Return the same way.

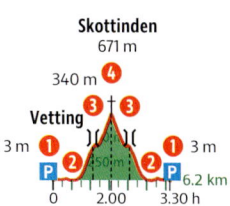

↗ 450m | ↘ 450m | 4.3km
2.30 hrs

20 Ballstadheia with Nonstinden, 459m

A wide open plateau at the southwestern tip of Vestvågøya

After a steep ascent you find yourself at the start of the extensive, gently ascending Ballstadheia. The grass and heath covered plateau extends from 200m up to 400m in altitude. The walk brings you all the way round the whole of the heia where you can wander at leisure and at a height of 459m you reach the summit of Nonstinden that marks the start of a jagged chain of mountains.

Starting point: Ballstad-Kræmmervika, car park, 10m. From Leknes, first follow the E 10 southwards (Leknes–Å) and continue the Fv 818 towards Ballstad. Just before you reach the end of the road, turn right into Kræmmervikveien and follow signs for Kræmmervika. Park a good 100m after the rorbuer settlement Kræmmervika Havn.
Grade: waymarked path, steep ascent (partly on natural stone steps) onto the heia, then a broad plain.
Infrastructure: accommodation, restaurants and supermarkets in Ballstad and Leknes. Petrol stations in Leknes.
Map: Vestvågøy.

There's still snow at 400m in spring.

From the car park in **Kræmmervika** ❶ follow the slowly ascending meadow path in a westerly direction that runs up between the stockfish racks. Now it's a constant and steep uphill climb on the mountain slope of the Ballstadheia, where the path gets increasingly rocky. You reach the edge of the mountain and come to a small stream that drains the plateau. At a **fork** ❷, continue in a westerly direction until you arrive at a **rocky promontory** ❸. Look down from here at the Nappstraumen far below and over to the island of Flakstadøya to the west.

On the heia.

A short detour can be followed along the paths running southwards over the rocky mountain ridge. Continue along this ridge to reach Brurstolen, 271m, the southernmost summit of Vestvågøya.

From the rocky promontory walk a short way back, then turn to the north and head towards a rock tower. Walk round this tower on the right hand side to reach a small col. From here it's just a short ascent across the meadowed slope onto the summit of **Nonstinden** ❹, 459 m.

A path, exposed in places, runs from here northwestwards as far as Munkan, 494m – another detour, but only for experienced mountain walkers.

From Nonstinden a steep path leads you back down the hillside to the heia where a myriad of paths run off in all directions. Orientate yourself along the broad well-trodden path at the northern edge of the mountain with airy views of the interior of Vestvågøya. The **Fløya** ❺ marks the northeastern edge of the plateau – Ballstad lies directly below you with its large port and shipyards.

From here it's a gentle descent across the meadowland to the **fork in the path** ❷ and then back down to **Kræmmervika** ❶.

↗ 180m | ↘ 180m | 5.1km
1.30 hrs

21 Hornsheia, 153m

An easy mountain with a beautiful and enchanting panorama

This path is one of the easiest walks on the Lofoten. After only a few vertical metres you are standing on a large and wonderful area of meadows and heathland. At the end of the ridge you come past the little forest of Nykan with its birch trees bent over by the wind and you are eventually rewarded with a panorama across Nappstraumen of the Flakstadøya mountain chain.

Starting point: walkers' car park near to Haug, 35m. Take the E 10 (Leknes–Å), 300m after the crossroads with the Fv 818 (Ballstad) follow the signpost to Haug (left), turn right at the next crossroads onto Haugveien, after 300m turn-off left onto a small gravel path. After 130m, a small car park is on the left.
Grade: easy walk on clearly defined path across meadowland.
Infrastructure: accommodation, restaurants, cafés, supermarkets and petrol stations in Leknes.
Map: Vestvågøy.

Haugheia and Hornsheia on the Offersøystraumen.

The little forest of Nykan.

From the **car park** ❶ follow the gravel path that ends after about 400m at a water tank. Continue the walk along a broad, well-trodden meadow path westwards. About 60m after walking through the pasture fence turn off the main path onto a small path to the right. Cairns act as waymarkers for your continuing path across the **Haugheia** ❷ as far as the **Hornsheia** ❸. From here the path turns in a southwesterly direction along the edge of the mountain to the elevation of Nykan with its fairytale little wood – a wonderful place to stop for a while and play. A good 450m further on your path ends at the **Horn** ❹, the southwesternmost elevation of the heia.

On your **return walk** pass the little wood on the right and continue in an easterly direction. This brings you back to the water tank again and to the gravel path that returns to the **car park** ❶.

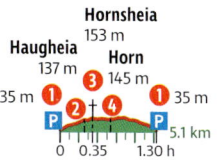

↗ 440m | ↘ 440m | 3.7km
2.30 hrs

22 Offersøykammen, 436m

A 'quick' viewpoint from Leknes and a mountain for training

Coming from Leknes, Offersøykammen lies directly before the Nappstraumen tunnel. It's the sole mountain on Offersøy, a small part of the island that is only connected by a small boggy land bridge with the main island of Vestvågøya. At the foot of Offersøykammen, in Sversvika bay, Neolithic excavations testify to the history of the early settlement along beside the tidal current of the Nappstraumen. From the summit you have a fascinating view of Vik bay with its white picture-book beaches of Haukland and Vik and also of the Himmeltindan massif.

Starting point: Skreda rest area, on the E 10, 20m. From Leknes follow the E 10 in the direction of Å, beforte the Nappstraumen tunnel.
Grade: well trodden, clear steep path with stony sections.
Infrastructure: accommodation, restaurants, cafés, supermarkets and petrol stations in Leknes.
Tip: do not miss a visit to Haukland beach (Walk 23).
Map: Vestvågøy.

Photo above: view towards Haukland.
Left: typical agricultural areas on Vestvågøya island.

From the **Skreda ❶** rest area walk along the E 10 towards Leknes for 600m. Here, you will find a well-trodden path at the left side of the road which is the **start ❷** of the actual summit climb. The path ascends through a small birchwood and you quickly gain height. The trees start to thin out and you are able to enjoy the panorama from Leknes over to Flakstad.
Eventually you reach the tree line and the path becomes less steep as it goes along a broad ridge to reach the summit of **Offersøykammen ❸**.
From here there is an incredibly striking view of the north coast of Flakstadøya and also of the picturesque Haukland beach.
Towards the south, you can see the long ridge of Hornsheia and Haugheia (Walk 21). With a little bit of patience you might be able to watch ptarmigan.
Return the same way to the **Skreda ❶** rest area.

↗ 230m | ↘ 230m | 8.1km

23 On old paths between Haukland and Utakleiv

2.15 hrs

Historical walk along a beautiful stretch of coastline

The paths that you walk on this circular walk have a colourful history. The old road over the pass has been there for a long time as the connecting route between Utakleiv and the rest of the world. In 1850 it was extended to make a horse and carriage track and in 1900 it was 2.5m wide, 6km long and had 17 bends. A replacement was sought for this tiresome route and from 1934 to 1947 a road was built around Veggen along the coast. There were 145 people living there at the time. The closure of the school in 1964 triggered an annual winter drama – the children rarely managed to get to school due to the fact that the Veggen road was often cut off. It was not until 1998 that the 899m long tunnel was built.

Starting point: Haukland, paid car park at the beach (with toilets), 10m. On the E 10 drive 4km north of Leknes, or southwest from Leknes on the E 10 following the sign for Haukland at the Offersøystraumen bridge.
Grade: easy walk with a moderate incline, stony on the pass. For the most part along old roadways.
Infrastructure: accommodation, restaurants, cafés, supermarkets and petrol stations in Leknes. Primitive campsite with water/toilets and paid car park in Utakleiv. Spending the night on Haukland beach is not allowed.
Alternative: walk in the opposite direction and/or begin your walk from the car park in Utakleiv.
Tips: Haukland is a paradise for sun worshippers and photographers. Those who come to watch the sunset or the midnight sun certainly will get their money's worth in Utakleiv.
You can also cycle along the coast following this route and at the end take a shortcut through the tunnel.
Map: Vestvågøy.

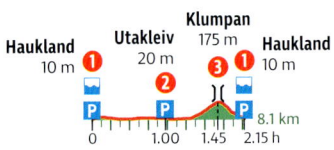

On the old road over the pass to Utakleiv.

From **Haukland beach** ❶ walk briefly in the direction of the road tunnel and turn left onto the gravel roadway. Soon you are heading for the small rocky island of Tåa which is only separated by a shallow strait. Below the huge steep rock face of Veggen continue on the old roadway built in 1947. With a bit of luck you can watch white-tailed eagles and porpoises. You can take advantage of the many benches along the way. After circling the entire massif, the wide Utakleiv valley opens out ahead and you are looking across to the steep rock faces of Medskolmen situated on the Steinsfjorden. As you arrive at the car park in **Utakleiv** ❷ you are greeted with the sight of a beautiful pebbly beach with shoreline terraces and the few farmhouses here while Himmeltindan (Walk 24) towers up above the valley. Continue your way as far as the tarmac road and turn right here. Shortly before the road tunnel take the roadway turning off left to the old school building of Utakleiv. You now find yourself on the old road over the pass dating back to 1850 which leads up several well constructed zigzags to the top of **Klumpan pass** ❸. Continue over a boggy area to reach the south side of the pass. In places along the following path you come across remains of the old supporting walls of the cart track which has been destroyed in places by landslides. Descend to a tarmac road and turn right. It's just a short way now back to the car park at **Haukland beach** ❶.

24 Himmeltindan, 931m

↗ 930m | ↘ 930m | 8.0km
4.30 hrs

Above the enchanting beaches on Vestvågøya

Himmeltindan is Vestvågøya's highest mountain. It consists of three peaks of which the largest is 964m high. It is however, in spite of its height, quite easily overcome. At its feet lie the wonderful beaches of Haukland and Utakleiv. The striking silhouette of Himmeltindan and also the gleaming silver radar tower of the NATO station on its summit are visible from a long way off. The main summit is a military exclusion zone and has been closed to walkers since the building of the radar station in 1984. The walk therefore finishes on one of the lower peaks. The station's staff does not have to use the hiking path, but are conveyed to the top by means of a lift inside the mountain.

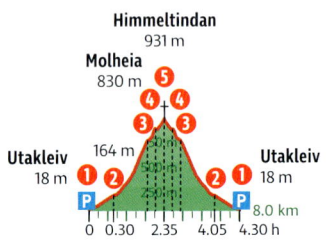

Right above: Himmeltindan with Utakleiv bay.
Below: view from Himmeltindan in the direction of Flakstadøya.

Starting point: Utakleiv, car park by the old school building, 18m. On the E 10 drive 4km north of Leknes respectively southwest from Leknes on the E 10 following the sign for Haukland at the Offersøystraumen bridge. After passing through the tunnel into Utakleiv valley an unsurfaced roadway turns off from the road on the right hand side. Follow this roadway to the former schoolhouse and park there. (For access see also the map for Walk 23.)
Grade: steep incline throughout on well defined, but unmarked mountain path, cairns in places.
Infrastructure: accommodation, restaurants, cafés, supermarkets and petrol stations in Leknes. Primitive campsite in Utakleiv. Spending the night on Haukland beach is not allowed.
Tips: at the end of the walk enjoy a refreshing swim in the Norwegian Sea: Haukland is considered Norway's most beautiful sandy beach.
The Lofotr Viking Museum (lofotr.no) is located in Borg and is well worth a visit. In the replica of the 83m long chieftain's house (the original excavation site is located just next to it) there's a beau-

tifully installed exhibition of everyday things which you are invited to touch and try. The modern museum building houses, amongst other things, an exhibition of relics and at the neighbouring Innerpollen you will find the replica of the famous Gokstad boat. A Viking festival takes places every summer and lasts several days.
Map: Vestvågøy.

On Utakleiv beach.

Start the walk from the old **Utakleiv** ❶ school building. (For more detail about Utakleiv's old connecting paths see Walk 23). Walk up the old road that leads to the Klumpan pass from where people once used to continue to Haukland. You come to a **boggy area** ❷ at the top of the pass where you see an obvious path turning off to the left. It is clearly waymarked at first with cairns and brings you northeastwards below Tuva, 450m, into the Durmålsdalen, a broad and steep valley. Ascend higher and higher up through the valley along beside extensive fields of blueberries. Below you can see the semi-circular arena of Utakleiv where the colourful houses are dotted around on the meadows like blobs of paint. From an altitude of 450m you are afforded your first mountain panorama stretching from the south to the southwest. At the end of the Durmålsdalen you arrive on a **hill** ❸ from where you can see the summit of Himmeltindan with its dominating radar station. The traces of your path become less obvious in this area and several more paths appear. Keep to the right, cross the hillside above Durmålsdalen for about 200m and then climb up onto **Molheia** hill ❹.

Then follows a short intermediary descent and after that a last pull up to the clearly visible 931m high summit of **Himmeltindan** ❺. You have now reached the objective of your walk and can enjoy a fantastic 360 degree view. Vestvågøya lies at your feet, in the northeast you can see across the Austlofoten as far as Vesterålen and in the southwest you will be able to spot the steep mountain peaks of Flakstadøya and Moskenesøya.
Return the same way to your starting point in **Utakleiv** ❶.

↗ 180m | ↘ 180m | 6.6km

2.30 hrs

Along the coastal path between Eggum and Unstad

25

Popular coastal walk at the time of the midnight sun

This walk is one of the most well known and popular walks on the Lofoten, especially at the time of the midnight sun. The use of a second car left at the end point, or a bicycle, is a practical alternative to walking there and back along the same route. We describe here the stretch from Eggum in the direction of Unstad. Unstad is definitely worth visiting with the beach and its surfers as this is the north Norwegian birthplace of this sport. The large waves do not actually occur until winter, but the small ones are high enough for starters and to have fun practising with a wet suit and surfboard.

Starting point: Tøan near Eggum, car park, 12m. On the E 10 in Bøstad turn off to Eggum, after 10km a toll road starts. There are no places to park here so drive on another 800m to Tøan.
End point: Unstad, car park at the community centre. Return with your second previously parked car or bike (distance by road Eggum–Unstad: 23km). Or on foot back the same way.
Grade: easy ('blue' walk) as far as the visitors' book ❸ then a demanding coastal path with stony and/or rocky sections, surefootedness necessary, extremely slippery when wet, cairns and T-waymarkers.

Infrastructure: caravan site and kiosque in Tøan (pay at the kiosque), campsite and café in Unstad. Accommodation, restaurants, cafés, supermarkets and petrol stations in Borg and Leknes.
Tips: surfing courses on offer from the surfers' campsite (unstadarcticsurf.com) and from the northernmost surf shop (lofotensurfsenter.no).
The ecological farm dairy of Marielle and Hugo is located in Saupstad between the two tunnels to Unstad. They sell tasty cheese, sausage and packed lunches and you can watch them making the cheese (lofoten-gardsysteri.no).
Map: Vestvågøy.

Unstad valley.

Walk right round the 'head' by M. Raetz where you will keep discovering something new.

In **Tøan** ❶ the remains of an old German radar installation from the Second World War can be found on a small hill. This is where your walk begins along a broad gravel track that at first leads you through the Eggum nature reserve with Nedre Heimredalsvatnet lake. The fascinating sculpture of **'The Head'** ❷ by Markus Raetz stands on a small hill and was erected in 1992 as part of the Skulpturlandskap Nordland project (skulpturlandskap.no). Continue now across the stony coastline where you will often see cormorants and sea eagles. From here you can already see Kleivheia navigational light on the horizon. After about 20 minutes the path brings you down to the pebble beach that is strewn with drift wood. At the end of the beach area you will find a **visitors' book** ❸. The more demanding

The coastal path between Eggum and Unstad.

part of the walk starts here. The path brings you alternately at sea level and across the higher sloping meadows. Especially beautiful are the two bays with round smooth stones. The path has slightly exposed sections, is repeatedly muddy and you have to negotiate some rock ledges. At last you climb up to **Kleivheia Fyr** ❹ navigational light. It's worth spending a bit of time here looking out for porpoises and orcas. On the way to the Kleivneset promontory the path is secured with chains, the ground is very loamy and the sheep droppings do not exactly make progress any easier. From **Kleivneset** you can already see Unstad. After a while you come to a pasture fence and an old roadway that leads you to the **Unstad** ❺ community centre behind a gate with places to park. Only another 10 minutes walk away you will come to Unstad campsite with a café where you can stop for a drink and a bite to eat.

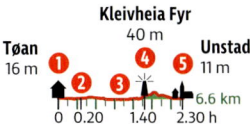

26 Steinetinden, 509m

↗ 860m | ↘ 860m | 8.3km
4.15 hrs

Exposed walk over the summit above Stamsund

The ridge walk over Kattberget and Mannfallet on Steinetinden is one of the most spectacular walks on the Lofoten. The challenging and airy walk offers fantastic views across the whole of the Vestfjorden as far as the islands of Mosken and Værøy. Directly below, you can see a multitude of skerries spread out between the individual parts of Vestvågøya island.

Starting point: Stamsund, Joker supermarket, 13 m, parking possible here.
Grade: unmarked, but good visible path, many steep and exposed sections (the path frequently runs along the edge of the ridge). The section of path from Steinetinden to Skredkollen is extremely steep in places (chains for protection). Surefootedness and a lack of vertigo are absolutely essential. The walk is to be avoided when wet.
Alternative: walk just to the summit of Steinetinden and return the same way in order to avoid the unspectacular return path in the area of the alpine ski complex.
Infrastructure: accommodation, restaurant, supermarket and petrol station in Stamsund.
Tips: from Kattberget (short ascent onto 173m, easy) there's a good view of Stamsund port where the Hurtigruten ships stop twice a day.
Stamsund is the fishing metropolis of the Lofoten. Otherwise the place is known for its rich cultural life with galleries, theatres and a theatre festival held every summer.
Map: Vestvågøy.

On the summit of Steinetinden – writing in the summit book is always a treat.

Follow the Ringveien road that starts opposite the supermarket in **Stamsund** ❶ for a few metres. Turn left at the next crossroads and join the Halsbakkan road which you follow towards the right above a residential area for 250m. Just before you reach a T-junction, there's the start of a stony and relatively boggy path (signposts) up the hillside of Kattberget. In 15 minutes you are standing on the **col** ❷ of the mountain ridge where this walk continues later. You are afforded your first fantastic view across the Vestfjorden from here. A short detour to the left onto **Kattberget** ❸ extends the panorama which you will continue to enjoy for the rest of the walk.

Back at the col follow the path westwards. At times exposed and steep, it runs over **Mannfallet** hill ❹. There's an intermediary descent across a broad meadowed ridge past birch trees bowed by wind and storms. From here you have an impressive view of Ureberget mountain, which is shaped like a hat, and a myriad of skerries lying in front.

About 270 vertical metres separate you from the summit of Steinetinden which you must overcome on a steep and sometimes exposed path. Below the summit structure an inscription marked in red on a rock indicates the way to the 'Topp' and to 'Heia', the continuation of the path. A short climbing passage over a rock ledge brings you onto **Steinetinden** ❺.

The shorter alternative descent route goes back the same way to Stamsund, but a longer route follows the continuing ridge. For this follow the sign for 'Heia' (there are red waymarker dots from here), descend the western mountain slope over extremely steep meadowland for about 100 vertical

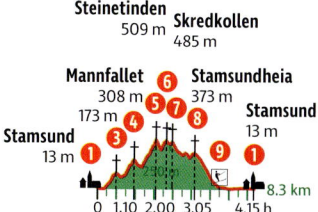

113

Steine's landscape of tiny islands.

metres where there are chains for protection and cross the hillside. The path now runs steeply uphill again, goes below the summit of **Ramntinden** ❻ and continues along the ridge as far as **Skredkollen** ❼. Afterwards continue along the western flank of the mountain, later on change over onto the eastern side to reach the **Stamsundheia** ❽. Descend the path beside the ski lift here that drops down to the **alpine centre** ❾ and follow the gravel road to the main Fv 817 road where you turn southwards and after 800m arrive back at your starting point at the supermarket in **Stamsund** ❶.

Alternatively, you could also follow the illuminated cross country ski track between the two lakes of Litl-Svarholtvatnet and Stor-Svarholtvatnet down to Ringveien street and then continue to the supermarket.

On the ridge between Ramntinden and Skredkollen.

↗ 840m | ↘ 840m | 12.6km

5.00 hrs

Justadtinden, 738m   27

Between rocks and peatlands

Justadtinden rises up above a totally wonderful hiking area. At 738m it brings you to quite a considerable height with wide views over the south-western part of the island of Vestvågøya and down to the Vestfjorden. The path runs across both lovely boggy and rocky terrain until you reach the Tjønnan lake area at 300m. Just walking up to this point is a worthwhile excursion for the whole family.

Starting point: Hagskaret pass, car park, 115m. From Leknes follow the Fv 815 (in the direction of Stamsund) for about 4km as far as Hagskaret pass, large car park on the left hand side.
Grade: long walk with a few very steep inclines (except in the summit area). Clearly visible path, some boggy sections.
Infrastructure: accommodation, restaurants, supermarkets and petrol stations in Leknes; campsites at Storfjordvatnet and Brustranda on the Fv 815.
Alternative: you could also do the walk in sections, e.g. with children. It's just 3.3km to the Tjønnan lake area; 4km onto Justadheia.
Tips: there are two small museums nearby that are open during the holiday season. The Skaftnes Gård Museum is a small farm of a typical fish farmer. From the Hagskaret car park, follow the Fv 815 in the direction of Stamsund and at the next crossroads turn right onto the Fv 7730, 7km to Skaftnes.
The Fygle Museum is located in an old school and also two old rorbuer. On display are the daily lives of fishermen as well as a former schoolroom with all its artifacts. Access from Hagskaret car park on the Fv 815, drive 2.6km towards Leknes, after the junction with the road to Mortsund (Fv 7730) there is a parking bay for the museum on the right hand side of the road.
Map: Vestvågøy.

Wetland cotton grass.

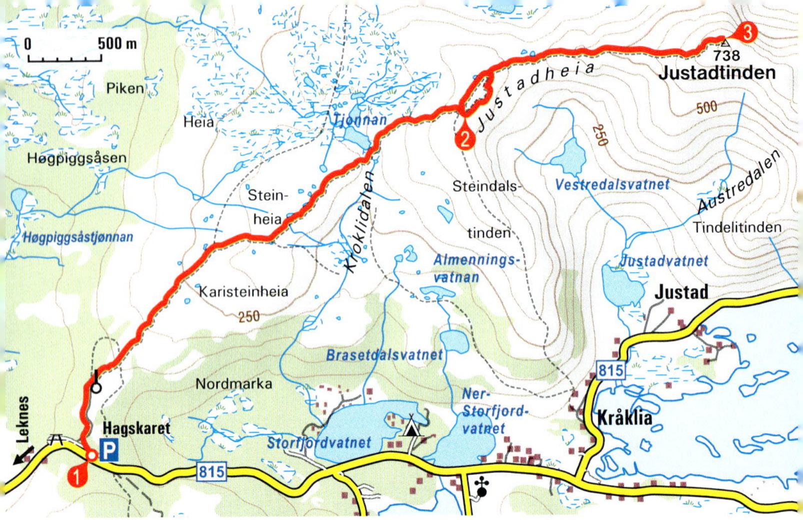

Start at the **Hagskaret** ❶ car park and follow the gravel road northwards to the mobile radio mast visible from a long way off. After a short while the roadway ends and you come to a well-trodden footpath that leads across boggy ground (wooden planks serve as bridges). After climbing the first few vertical metres you can see a long way across Vestvågøya towards Leknes. Soon you reach a dry area with dwarf birch trees and short shrubby willows. The path leads you eastwards between the highest peaks of Steinheia, 352m, and the Karisteinheia, 342m. The terrain becomes increasingly stony and rocky. Now head east around the Steinheia and into the large boggy depression where the Tjønnan lake area begins. Walk again over planks, past cotton grass and cloudberries.

After the depression, walk up the **Justadheia** ❷ until you reach its steeply sloping eastern flank. Far below are the lakes of Vestredalsvatnet and Justadvatnet and also the hamlet of Justad. To the south the steep ridge runs all the way to **Steindalstinden** (Kroklitinden), 464m. If you like, finish your walk here, find a comfy spot and watch the sea eagles.

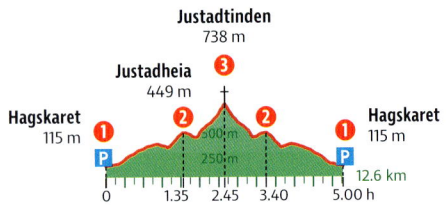

116

Now continue northeastwards on your way to Justadtinden. On a short intermediary descent, pass the Moshumpan col from where you gain the western flank which leads you across rocky and repeated sections of grass-covered terrain to the summit. A last short, but steep climb takes you to the summit rock of **Justadtinden** ❸. Up here, you are greeted by a breathtaking view of the majestic Vågakallen which towers beyond the Hennings-værstraumen. This all-round view of the Lofoten is certainly rewarding: a patchwork of mountains, water and islands opens up below you.
Return along the same path to the **starting point** ❶.

Boggy landscape at Tjønnan lake.

↗ 360m | ↘ 360m | 5.9km
2.15 hrs

28 Brattflogan, 460m

In the centre of Vestvågøya

This varied walk brings you onto Brattflogan that lies in the heart of Vestvågøya. There are several paths that lead to the extensive fen with lots of cotton grass, blueberries and cloudberries before finally reaching the inconspicuous summit. Inspite of its modest height, you will be able to enjoy the beautiful panorama and appreciate this quiet and remote location, especially when the midnight sun is up.

Starting point: Slydalen, car park at the end of the roadway, 155m. 1.5km south of the Viking Museum in Borg, from the E 10 turn onto the toll gravel road (sign: Slydalen, Skytebane) and follow this for 3km; not suitable for camper vans.
Grade: this is a easy walk with gentle inclines. Orientation and route finding can be a bit tricky at times across the fen and heathland. There are a few cairns in places.

Infrastructure: Brustranda campsite with café on the Fv 815. Supermarkets in Borg and Leknes, petrol stations in Leknes.
Alternative: access onto Brattflogan from Brustranda campsite on the Fv 815; the exact description see p. 120.
Tip: horse rides can be booked in Valberg, 1km east of Brustranda (lofothest.no).
Map: Vestvågøy.

Studying the map on Brattflogan.

Start your walk from the car park in the **Slydalen valley** ❶, follow the old agricultural path and pass an information board and a sheep fence. After about 200 metres a clearly visible path waymarked with blue sticks turns off left and ascends the slope.

30 minutes later you arrive at a **high plateau** ❷ with large boggy areas. In early summer it can be quite difficult to find the path here in places, but a few cairns and the mountain ridge of Brattflogan lying to the west aid your orientation.

Walk along the south side past the lake of **Stortjønna**. After crossing the boggy area it's a gentle ascent diagonally across the hillside up to a faintly defined col. Once you reach the col follow the tiny path to the right to the rocky summit elevation of **Brattflogan** ❸.

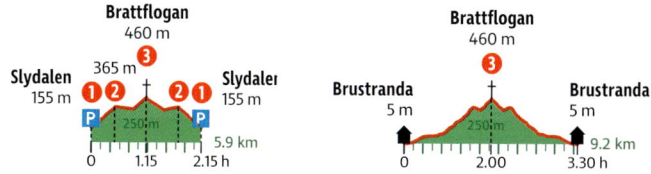

Just a temporary residence in Slydalen.

Return the same way to your starting point, but due to the many sheep tracks in this area you really need to take care: on the large boggy high plateau walk past the lake of Stortjønna again. Shortly afterwards the path makes a 90 degree turn to the right where there's a large cairn. You now need to follow this path. The sheep track heading straight on would lead you into the Steinbakkelva valley.

Alternative: ascent from **Rolvsfjorden** (3.30 hrs, 520 vertical metres, a 'red' walk; starting point is Brustranda on the Fv 815, parking at the former petrol station/car repair garage, 5m)
Start from the entrance to **Brustranda campsite** and follow the Fv 815 for about 100m northeastwards. A gravel track turns off here on the left hand side which brings you into **Tjønndalen**. After 1.5km the roadway changes at the last house in Tjønndalen into a soggy, loamy meadow path. After 350m you come to a fork in the path where you turn left (sign: Vendalsjorden). You gradually gain height along an old mule path and overcome a stepped and undulating grass-covered boggy landscape. Ascend a hill and the valley of Vendalsjorden soon comes into view on your right hand side.

The route finding now becomes difficult (few cairns and some sheep tracks). The path forks at one point: the clearly visible and well-trodden path (left) runs gently up the hillside in a southwesterly direction. However, take the tiny track on the right hand side which leads towards a cairn at the mountain's edge above Vendalsjorden valley. You meet a path here that runs along the edge. Turn left and ascend the mountain ridge. On your right hand side you are accompanied by the view down to the Vendalsjorden and of Borgpollen. On the left hand side you can look down towards Tjønndalen with views of both the Rolvsfjorden and the Vestfjorden. You come to a large sandy area (where the sheep lie down). There are two options here: either carry straight on up a steep incline onto a broad ridge which then leads you to the end of the high valley of Djupdalen lying on your left below. Or, you can follow a sheep track to the left that brings you up a gentle incline to the start of the high valley of **Djupdalen**.

An elongated stretch of peatland awaits you at this point with countless cotton grass plants. Walk along the northern side of this boggy area into the valley and at the end of the valley you meet up with the path again that was the first option. Cross the boggy area to climb up the mountain hillside opposite to the col. Once you have arrived at the col follow the tiny track to the left to the rocky summit elevation of **Brattflogan** ❸.
Return the same way to the **starting point** ❶.

Having fun in the wind on Brattflogan mire.

↗ 420m | ↘ 420m | 5.1km

29 Vetten, 414m

2.00 hrs

Easy walk to the Aalan Gård

The walk across Vetten or even just the ascent of the summit from Lauvdalen is a lovely walk for the whole family and not too difficult. Since the ascent is not that high, you can also enjoy a beautiful view when the cloud is low.

Starting point: car park at Borgfjord, community centre, 22m, on the E 10. 3.4km northeast of the Viking Museum in Borg, shortly after the turn-off to Vendalsjord, turn right onto a gravel road and into the car park for the community centre. Alternative parking can be found 380m further on at Torvdalshalsen service area and viewpoint.
End point: Aalan Gård goat farm in the Lauvdalen. Return either on foot or on the bike that you left there before the walk on the gravel road in Lauvdalen and the FV 7608 road (4.5km).
Grade: easy, clearly visible path over heathland, waymarking with cairns and signposts.
Infrastructure: accommodation, restaurants, cafés, supermarkets and petrol stations in Borg and Leknes. Aalan Gård goat farm/dairy with summer café (aalan.no) where you can buy cheese, herbs and tea.
Alternative: start from the Aalan Gård farm, make the ascent of Vetten and return to the farm.
Map: Vestvågøy.

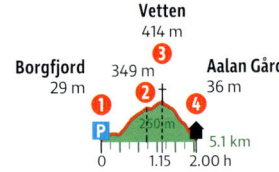

Start the walk from the car park at the **Borgfjord** ❶ community centre along the path running northwards across the meadows and heathland. Continue up the gentle incline and the alternative approach from Torvdalshalsen col joins from the left. The path winds its way over even ground southeastwards before you turn northeastwards up the slope onto the large high plateau of Helfjellet. Looking south and southwest you can see into the centre of Vestvågøya, while in the northwest can be seen the northernmost tip of the island with Haveren, 808m.

Soon you come past the **junction** ❷ with the path that turns northwards up to the prominent rock of Finnkjerka, 392m. Now it's just another few hundred metres to the summit of **Vetten** ❸ which is strewn with boulders. Below you can see the lakes, pollen, inlets and tidal currents where the Vikings of the court of Borg had their home long ago and if you look carefully, you can see the large Viking house at the Lofotr Viking Museum in the distance.

The descent leads over a narrow ridge that brings you to Nubben, a rocky elevation with a steep southwest facing hillside. The path goes round a sharp left hand bend here and you walk towards the southern end of the level and boggy Gongskaret col. Having arrived on the col you now need to turn southwards. The route finding is more difficult with many different paths through the tall grass. Finally you reach an old roadway that zigzags down to the **Aalan Gård** ❹ farm, a lovely place to linger with coffee, cheese, cake and waffles.

For your **return** walk westwards along the gravel road and turn right at the next junction (4.5km, 1 hr). This 4.5km stretch can be made much easier if you are able to leave a bike at the farm beforehand.

The Aalan Gård goat farm in the Lauvdalen.

30 Haveren, 808m

↗ 820m | ↘ 820m | 8.3km
3.45 hrs

Onto the highest mountain in the north of Vestvågøya

Between Sandøya and Eggum lies the small island group of Borgvær, as the last post to the open Norwegian Sea, on which egg and down collecting was an important source of income. The main island with the same name was inhabited until 1960 and played an important role in the past as a trading hub. Until the First World War Borgvær was the most southern island dealing in the so called Pomor trade, which was practised by the Pomors, an ethnic group from the White Sea. Already in Viking times trade was conducted with Russia via the northern sea route. From then on until the 17th century there was a lively exchange with the Sami living on the coast. And from the year 1740 onwards the Pomor trade expanded along Norway's northern coast. The Russian ships coming from the White Sea region brought rye flour (Russian flour), dairy products, salt, wood and much more, in exchange for fish. The ruble became the currency in many places and Russenorsk, a kind of Russian-Norwegian pidgin language was developed. After the October Revolution the Pomor trade came to a standstill.

View up to the summit.

Starting point: Bø, parking bay after the village name sign (at a passing place opposite the radio mast), 40m. From the E 10 (coming from Leknes) the Haverringen road turns off left on a steep right hand bend; signs for Kvalnes as well as Skolestua and Kolonial/Food; 3.7km to the parking bay.

Grade: this is a demanding walk where the paths are not always clear, sometimes across heathland or through woods, sometimes boggy, in the upper area stony, sections of scree. Exposed summit ridge. Total lack of vertigo essential. Cairns in the upper area.

Infrastructure: along the Haverringen road (Fv 7728) Restaurant Skolestua Gjestegård, Restaurant Am Havern (sumptuous Sunday buffet) and accommodation. Summer café at the Aalan Gård goat farm and dairy (aalan.no) in the Lauvdalen. Accommodation, restaurants and petrol stations in Leknes; supermarkets in Borg and Leknes.

Alternative: an alternative start runs from the car park along the road to Bø. After about 920m you will see a red building on the left and a passing place on the right hand side of the road. A path begins from here over the meadows along beside the pasture fence as far as the bank of moraine ❷ on Bøvatnet lake (Dalvatnet). If you decide to start from here, or use it for your return, it bypasses the heathland and avoids the boggy wooded area.

Tips: the Lofotr Viking Museum is located in Borg which has an interesting exhibition in the replica of the largest Viking house which has ever been found

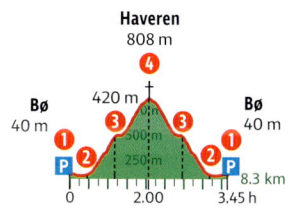

in northern Norway and is well worth a visit.

The countless islands close to the coast right up to Borgvær provide a lovely place for paddle boarding.

Map: Vestvågøy.

Your walk starts at the car park in **Bø** ❶. A narrow path leads you across a heath-covered landscape directly towards the mountain of Litlhaveren, 471m, lying ahead. After a good 100m you pass a gate in the pasture fence and immediately afterwards meet a cross path which you follow to the left. You are soon walking through a little wood with dwarf birch trees. The route finding is a bit tricky here as the path is not clearly visible and boggy. After about 400m you come onto open heathland again and in the northwest you can see the small settlement of Bø. The path once more becomes clearly visible here and leads you onto a sloping hill, a **bank of moraine** ❷. Bøvatnet lake (Dalvatnet) lies beyond the moraine.

Turn right here. The Litlhaveren massif lies ahead. Your path leads you uphill into the Trolldalen hanging valley on the left of the massif. It becomes stonier underfoot and you pass a scree slope and afterwards cross the steeply ascending hillside through a dwarf birch forest and heathland. Looking back you can see Bø and the offshore islands of Sandøya. On the right below you lies the long extended Bøvatnet lake and opposite, the mountain slope of Middagstinden, 707m. As you continue your ascent keep right and climb onto the **high plateau** ❸ ahead which is covered

in sparse vegetation. Once you have reached the plateau you have the option of taking a short detour to the right onto the rocky summit **Litlhaveren**, 471m.

Turn to the left and head towards the broad ridge of Haveren lying ahead. The path loses itself somewhat here, but further on it becomes clear again. On your ascent you have a view on the right hand side of Vestresand and the mountain massif in the distance near Eggum. The small archipelago of Borgvær lies off the coast of Vestresand. The path becomes increasingly stony and you even have to make your way across areas of scree in places. Cairns guide you along the way here. A large steinvarden (cairn) stands on the plateau before Haveren.

Now the exposed section along the jagged ridge lies ahead of you. You overcome the last airy 40 vertical metres before reaching the summit of **Haveren** ❹ at 808m. Your 360 degree view extends across the mountains of Vestvågøya and the Norwegian Sea. In suitable weather conditions you can see the high Vågakallen at Henningsvær on Austvågøya. Hoven is unmistakable as it stands in its solitary location on the bogs on Gimsøya island. **Return** along the same path back to the **starting point** ❶.

Photo above: on the high plateau with a view of the Middagstinden massif.
Left: view across Urvatnet lake and the islands around Borgvær.

31 — Hoven, 368m

TOP

↗ 380m | ↘ 380m | 3.9km
1.45 hrs

Shark's fin in the bogs of Gimsøya

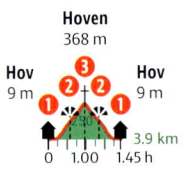

The island of Gimsøya lies between Austvågøya and Vestvågøya and is accessed via the E 10 over the Gimsøystraumenbrua and Sundklakkstraumenbrua bridges. The southern part of the island, only 46.4km² in size, is dominated by a massif whose peaks tower steeply up to a height of 767m. In the northern part of the island, on the other hand, old coastlines and bogs with different structures and types of vegetation predominate. 6400 hectares of these are under conservation including a raised bog unique in its kind in northern Norway. The easily accessible Hoven rises up like a shark's fin north of the boggy areas. A lovely family walk along its foot is probably Norway's most beautifully situated golf course.

Midnight sun on Hoven.

View of the coastline from the summit.

Starting point: Hov, paid car park at the golf course, 9m. Follow the signs from the E 10.
Grade: moderately strenuous walk. A small bog to be crossed at the start. Short sections with steep ledges. Be careful on the summit – steeply falling west flank, usually very windy.
Infrastructure: café and accommodation at the golf course, campsite and holiday homes in Hov (lofotenlinks.no). Supermarket and petrol station in Vinje.
Tips: it is especially good fun to play golf during the midnight sun on Gimsøy (lofotenlinks.no) – and only a few hundred metres to the west lies the wonderful beach of Hovsvika.
Map: Vågan.

The flat boggy landscape around Hoven.

Start from the large gravel car park for the golf course in **Hov** ❶. From here you can clearly see the elongated ridge of Hoven over which you will ascend. From the western end of the car park walk along a roadway to a small warehouse and you will find the start of a narrow path behind it that leads southwards through the boggy area.

After 15 minutes the path turns southwest and you start to climb up the ridge. 20 minutes after that you reach a small **high plateau** ❷, from where you are afforded a beautiful view down to Hovsvika bay with its white sandy beach.

Over soft terrain strewn with dwarf heathers continue uphill for another 40 minutes until you reach the summit of the **Hoven** ❸. Be careful at the summit edge as the mountain slopes drop steeply towards the sea at this point! From here there's a beautiful panoramic view along the outer edge of the Lofoten up to Vesterålen, and also of the boggy areas below.

Return the same way to the **starting point** ❶.

↗ 560m | ↘ 560m | 3.9km

3.00 hrs

Festvågtinden, 541m | 32

Henningsvær from above

A steep ascent leads to a terrace at the foot of Festvågtinden in the climbing area near Henningsvær. The lake of Heiavatnet is located here, the former water supply to Henningsvær. For those walkers who prefer not to climb Festvågtinden there's already a beautiful view from here of the 'Venice of Lofoten' – Henningsvær. Another option is a walk around the small lake. A magnificent view over the Vestfjorden awaits those who manage to climb onto the summit.

Starting point: Festvåg, car park on the Fv 816 by the buildings on the right hand side, 5m. Further parking on the left before the first bridge to Henningsvær. Both car parks are subject to a fee.
Grade: very steep, sandy path with sections of scree, difficult route finding at the rocky start of the climb, exposed summit area, surefootedness and a lack of vertigo are absolutely essential.
Infrastructure: accommodation, cafés, restaurants and supermarket in Henningsvær. Petrol stations in Svolvær. Campsite on the Lyngværsundet, also in Rystad on the Fv 7628.
Tips: Festvågtinden stands in the middle of a popular climbing area west of Vågakallen. The walk on Vågakallen is a demanding and strenuous full day trip for experienced mountain walkers (a 'black' walk, information: climbing school, Nord Norsk Klatreskole in Henningsvær).
A leisurely stroll through the old fishing village of Henningsvær with its interesting galleries and cafés is highly recommended.
Map: Vågan.

Henningsvær port in winter.

The view below of Henningsvær's offshore islands.

Start at the car park in **Festvåg** ❶ and walk about 250m along the surfaced road towards Henningsvær and along beside Urvika bay right to the end. A well-trodden path leads from here under trees up some stone steps beside the remnants of the wall of Henningsvær's former water supply. Afterwards the path winds its way between large fragments of broken rock over a scree slope. But after about only 20m you need to leave the well-trodden path that leads northwards towards the climbing walls at the foot of the Festvågtind massif. Turn right and find your way along a tiny, not very obvious path between the boulders. At the end of this labyrinth of stone you meet a path that leads northeastwards steeply up the valley. At a **height of 130m** ❷ the path forks and continues to the right onto the high plateau with Heiavatnet lake (your return route). Take the left hand path here and work your way up the very steep hillside. The path is unrelenting as it continues to ascend until at about 520m, you finally reach a broad mountain ridge. Now head southwestwards towards the rocky summit area and with a valiant effort and use of your hands, you are eventually standing on the summit of **Festvågtinden** ❸.

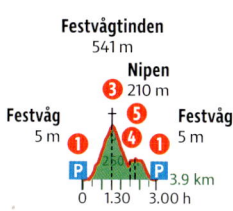

On the descent follow the same route at first, but then do not descend the steep mountain hillside down into the valley, but orientate your self towards the high plateau and follow the clearly visible path down to **Heiavatnet lake** ❹, the old Henningsvaer reservoir for drinking water. This is a popular bathing spot especially on warm days. Various tiny tracks bring you to very different viewpoints. The path heading southwestwards onto the **Nipen** ❺ is particularly worth the effort.

In order to return to Festvåg look for one of two paths that lead steeply down along the edge of the plateau to join your initial ascent route and continue back down to the car park in **Festvåg** ❶.

Atlantic white-sided dolphin in the Vestfjorden.

↗ 400m | ↘ 400m | 5.8km
2.15 hrs

33 Glomtinden, 419m

A popular mountain

An attractive walk for the young and old. The ascent is easy to accomplish and from Rørvikskaret you are wandering through a magical rocky landscape where you can enjoy clambering about or stopping for a rest. Braver souls can climb up onto the summit which stands in the shadow of Vågakallen like a fortress.

Starting point: Rørvikvatnet, parking bay on the northern side of the E 10 at the start of the old road over the pass, 42m. Coming along the E 10 from Svolvær it can be found after the Rørvik tunnel on the right hand side. Coming from Vestvågøy it's 600m after the crossroads E 10/Fv 816 (Henningsvær). Further parking can be found in Rørvika.
Grade: easy, well-walked path with short steeper sections.
Infrastructure: camping and accommodation as well as cafés, restaurants and supermarkets in Kabelvåg, Henningsvær and Svolvær. Petrol stations in Svolvær. Simple campsite on Kalle beach. There are campsites on the Lyngværsundet between Rørvika and Gimsøya, also in Rystad on the Fv 7628.
Alternative: descent with beautiful views towards the Vestfjorden across the narrow eastern ridge to the Hopspollen. The path is exposed in places over the ridge and stone slabs (350 vertical metres, 45 mins, a 'red' walk). However, for your return to the car park you will either need a bicycle or a second car.
Tip: Rørvika beach with its white sand and turquoise-blue water becomes a popular bathing spot on warm days.
Map: Vågan.

High above the Rørvikvatnet.

On the summit of Glomtinden.

From the parking bay at **Rørvikvatnet lake** ❶ follow the old road over the pass as far as **Rørvikskaret col** ❷. A large hole with a fence around it is the evidence of a rockfall during the building of the road tunnel in the 1970s. The footpath turns off here to the right. A confusing number of paths run across the stony and sandy terrain in places. On a 300m high hill you pass a small area of rocks where you can find some ideal spots to stop for a rest and play. The path continues up along the mountain ridge to a **hill** ❸ with a fantastic view of the Vestfjorden. You can finish your walk here. The rocky summit on the right hand side has the appearance of a castle. Those walkers who feel brave enough, can overcome the last few metres to the top of **Glomtinden** ❹ up a steep and sandy path through boulders. **Return** the same way to **Rørvikvatnet** ❶ on the E 10.

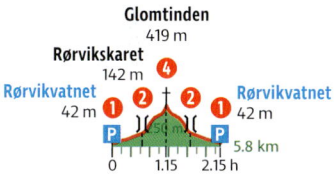

↗ 390m | ↘ 390m | 5.4km
2.30 hrs

34 Tjeldbergtinden, 367m

Imposing mountain between Svolvær and Kabelvåg

Although the oystercatchers are the inspiration for its name, Tjeldbergtinden also has the appearance of a table mountain. This isolated mountain rises up above Svolvær. After a quick ascent this nippy little walk offers lovely views across this small 'metropolis' and Kabelvåg, and a beautiful vista of the mainland and Vågakallen right opposite.

Starting point: Osan, Kongsvatnveien, 15 m. Along the E 10 from Svolvær in the direction of Kabelvåg, on the right opposite the Osan ship-building yard. Parking at the Esso petrol station or at the KIWI supermarket.
Grade: an easy walk for the most part, the ascent of the eastern flank leads via a very steep zigzag path.
Infrastructure: accommodation and camping, cafés, restaurants and supermarkets in Kabelvåg and Svolvær. Petrol stations in Svolvær.
Tips: from the southeastern tip ❺ of Tjeldbergtinden you can watch the Hurtigruten ships arriving at Svolvær (southern departure 18.30, northern departure 21.20).
The picturesque village of Kabelvåg is an attractive place for a stroll.
In Storvågan you can visit the Lofoten Aquarium and the Lofoten Museum. The interesting Galleri Espolin with works by the artist Kaare Espolin Johnson gives a very strong impression of the harsh rigour of life in the far north and of Lofoten fishing.
Map: Vågan.

View to the summit of Tjeldbergtinden.

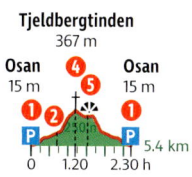

From the petrol station in **Osan** ❶ walk along the Kongsvatnveien road for just under 200m northwestwards and then turn left into a side road. On the left hand bend after a good 70m take the gravel road that runs straight ahead (barrier). Walk up the roadway and you come past the 'Tjeldbergtind Skytebane' shooting range. The gravel road leads further uphill to a mobile phone mast on Tjeldbergaksla hill. Unfortunately, tall bushes obscure the view somewhat from here.

Turn off to the right at a large **boulder** ❷ (wooden sign) at the edge of the path. The footpath now narrows, but continues as a clearly visible path through a birchwood. At the end of this path you find yourself standing before the eastern flank of the mountain which you now need to overcome on a winding and arduous path uphill. A sea of blueberries lines the path here. Once you arrive at the top of the ridge turn first left and at the following **junction** ❸ walk to the right, at first heading towards the blocky summit of **Tjeldbergtinden** ❹. You can climb onto the top directly from the

View of Vågakallen, 943m.

front or from the left hand side. However, a particularly spectacular view awaits you from the southeastern **tip of the mountain massif** ❺ above the E 10 and the bay of Tjeldbergvika.

Return down the same path as far as the **junction** ❸ and continue back to the car park in **Osan** ❶.

↗ 510m | ↘ 510m | 4.5km

35 Tuva, 477m

2.15 hrs

🚌 👫

Family walk in Svolvær

Tuva is a lovely alternative to the more difficult Fløya (Walk 36). There are impressive views from here, too, across Svolvær and the Vestfjorden. On the way there are secluded little spots for a picnic by Grønnåsvatnet lake so that this walk is an ideal choice for a family outing. More experienced walkers have the option of extending the walk by making an ascent of the more difficult Blåtinden at an altitude of 625m.

the turn-off from the Villaveien to the Feriesenter.
Grade: signposted, clearly visible footpath; boggy sections with some wooden planks for bridges at times. Rocky sections – be careful here when it's wet.
Infrastructure: accommodation and camping, also restaurants, supermarkets and petrol stations in Svolvær, information at the tourist office in the marketplace.
Alternative: there's the option of an extension to the walk with a detour onto Blåtinden (see the description below).
Tip: Svolvær (4500 inhabitants) is the largest town on the Lofoten and is consequently a busy centre. Attractions here are the Lofoten War Memorial Museum, the Magic Ice (ice sculpture exhibition and bar), galleries, ferry dock for the Hurtigruten line and ferries to the island of Skrova, also to Skutvik and Bodø. In summer you can take a sea eagle safari or a boat trip on the Trollfjorden (information: visitlofoten.com and at the tourist information in the marketplace).
Map: Vågan.

Starting point: Svolvær, car park at the Red Cross building (Røde Kors), 12m. At the yacht marina (where there are two petrol stations opposite one another) turn off the E 10 onto the side road and follow the sign to the Lofoten Feriesenter. The small Sommartjønna lake and the Red Cross building are located at

From the car park in **Svolvær** ❶ follow the surfaced road further northwards. On the sharp right hand bend a private gravel road turns off to the left. On the right above this road, steeply up the wooded hillside, is located a large wooden sign with the names 'Blåtinden' and 'Tuva'.
Ascend this steep and extremely well-trodden path over tree roots. Very soon the at first muddy and loamy ground underfoot alternates with

The summit within touching distance.

smooth rock. After a few vertical metres you can look back for views across parts of Svolvær and the Vestfjorden while to the southwest you will be able to see the imposing summit ridge of Tjeldbergtinden, 367m (Walk 34) and also the majestic, 943m high Vågakallen beyond. Looking ahead you will see from right to left in the distance Fløya, 590m, Blåtinden, 625m, and your final destination, Tuva.

Continue along the path through light birch trees as far as the built-up **Grønnåsvatnet lake** ❷ which you walk around on the left hand (western) side. The trees become much denser again here.

On your way you cross over several small stone dams. After the last dam, with a small overflow, you arrive at a beautiful picnic spot.

Continue across wooden planks that serve as a bridge towards the valley ahead. Now go uphill again across lighter terrain. The nature of the path varies between rocky, stony and

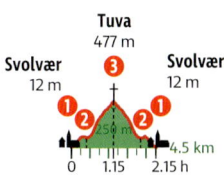

On the ridge of Blåtinden.

muddy sections. A little stream with small waterfalls accompanies you for a while on the right hand side. You now come above the treeline into a boggy area. Here too there are wooden planks to help you across some wetter areas. The path leads you in the direction of the col between Blåtinden and Tuva. Once you arrive at the col you will see Tuvvatnet lake located in a cirque. Turn left here and climb up along the narrow ridge to the rocky summit of **Tuva** ❸. A short climbing section to the top can be avoided by walking around the steep slope on the right.

Return the same way to the **starting point** ❶.

Alternative: detour onto Blåtinden, 625m (250 vertical metres, 1 hr from the col, a 'red' walk; in the summit area 'black', clearly visible path, some blue and white waymarkers)

From the top of Tuva you can clearly see the path onto Blåtinden. In order to reach this path, descend from Tuva back down to the col and after that follow your ascent path for another 100m until you come to an obvious cairn. A path turns off left here that brings you up the slope onto a small hill. After roughly a further 100m you cross a scree slope to then climb a mountain ridge lying to the right of the slope. This brings you more steeply up to the main ridge of **Blåtinden** where you ascend to a first wonderful viewpoint with views towards Vestfjorden. Then there's still a short easy section to go before the last vertical metres to the **summit**, 625m, which should only be attempted by experienced climbers.

↗ 640m | ↘ 640m | 4.2km
3.00 hrs

Fløya, 590m | 36

Local peak with Svolværgeita, the landmark of Svolvær

Svolværgeita located at the southwestern side of Fløya is a pinnacle over 100m high that has two 'horns', hence the name 'Svolvær goat'. It is a well-known rock for climbers and on the descent from Storhorn they jump across a 1.5m wide gap (a popular photo opportunity) to land safely onto Lillehorn from where there's a view down onto Svolvær cemetery lying 300m below. On the exposed ascent to Fløya you come past Djevelporten, 'devil's gate', which is a large rock slab that is wedged into a crevice and a little less scary place in which to have your photo taken.

Starting point: Svolvær, northwestern corner of Blåtindveien, big paid car park above the nursery school, 10m. In Svolvær follow the E 10 (towards Narvik) and after the harbour/marina turn left into Nyveien, turn right another twice, then left into Blåtindveien.
Grade: blue and white waymarked footpath with natural stone steps (sherpasti), rocky sections and scree. Attention: recommended for experienced and sure-footed mountain walkers with a good head for heights, scrambling sections in the summit area. Be especially careful when wet.
Infrastructure: accommodation and camping, also restaurants, supermarkets and petrol stations in Svolvær.
Tip: Svolvær, see Walk 35.
Map: Vågan.

On the Djevelporten.

The first few metres from the walkers' car park in **Svolvær** ❶, are on a gravel path which quickly leads you to the steep stone steps that were built by some Sherpas. The steps take you through a small boulder field past rowan and birch trees up the slope in front of you. From here, you can clearly see the Svolværgeita, and with every step higher the view of Svolvær opens below and across to Vestfjorden. There are several small stone benches along the way to rest, and you can enjoy a magnificent view from a larger **rest area** ❷.

Once you reach an altitude of 200m, you have overcome the steep slope and walk towards a hanging valley. At a **junction** ❸, the approach to Svolværgeita turns off to the right. Follow the signs towards Fløya. The stone steps are becoming less frequent, and the path now leads across rocks and through boggy sections which are equipped with a boardwalk. After a rocky elevation, the path is covered in scree and takes you towards the karst peak

of Frosken (frog, 495m) that lies ahead of you. You can see the Djeveltrappa (devil's stairs) on the flank of the Frosken which ascends to the Djevelporten col (you will take this path on the way back). Just before the start of the steps, follow the signs to Fløya at a **turn-off** ❹ to the right. The path leads up the slope to the **summit ridge** ❺ that stretches between the summit of Fløya and its fore summit. The path is very steep – covered in scree in the lower section and with a peaty surface in the upper area (be careful not to slip here). After you have climbed up to the ridge, you can walk onto its **fore summit** ❻ to the right before making your final ascent of the main summit, from where you can enjoy a full view across Svolvær. The last few metres to the summit of **Fløya** ❼ should only be tackled by walkers with climbing experience.

For your **return** take the path below the summit structure that heads northwards and descends the steep mountain slope to the **Djevelporten** ❽. From here, take the Djeveltrappa to descend to the hanging valley which you know already. From the **turn-off** ❹ that you took to reach Fløya return the same way to the walkers' car park in **Svolvær** ❶.

Descent with Svolværgeita (left).

↗ 520m | ↘ 520m | 9.5km
3.00 hrs

37 Walking on the island of Skrova

Old whalecatchers' island in the Vestfjorden

Skrova was, into the last century, one of the largest fishing villages in the Lofoten. Alongside Lofoten fishing in winter, whale catching was an important line of business. There are about 190 people still living on Skrova today. The main occupation of the people living here these days is, first and foremost, aquaculture. A walk on Skrova is a beautiful whole day trip for the whole family if you include the ferry crossings, the many stops for a rest and photo opportunities.

Starting point: Heimskrova, ferry dock on the island of Skrova, 3m, regular ferry service from Svolvær (torghatten-nord.no).
Grade: waymarked footpath with moderate inclines. A chain-protected section on the ascent to Høgskrova.
Infrastructure: small supermarket in the village, Heimbrygga (restaurant and accommodation, heimbrygga.no). A converted old oil tank offers a spectacular place to stay (oljetanken.no).
Tips: the path is also an easy walk for less experienced walkers if you don't include the climb onto the top of Høgskrova.
The water around Skrova, the islands of Litlmolla, Stormolla and Årsteinen, Raftsundet too are excellent places for taking a sea kayak trip.
Map: Vågan.

When you come by ferry from Svolvær you disembark at **Heimskrova** ❶ ferry dock onto the most densely populated part of the Skrova group of islands. The main road leads into the northeasternmost part of the island before crossing a breakwater southwestwards towards the main island. The surfaced road

In Skrova harbour.

The island of Skrova.

runs to the end of the Kuholmen. Here, in a tunnel, you'll find an interesting **photo exhibition** ❷ about life on Skrova.

350m back along the road a large board indicates the network of paths on the island. Follow a gravel path (in winter an illuminated cross-country ski run) to the east to **Hattvika bay** ❸ where you can cool off with a swim in warm weather.

Leave the bay along the same path. After about 300m the blue waymarked path turns off to the left and ascends in the direction of Høgskrova massif. 50 vertical metres later you leave the broad well-worn path that leads to the summit and orientate yourself along the the narrow path that runs southwards onto a small **col** ❹ between Høgskrova (right) and a small

Along the outer eastern edge of Skrova past Nautøya bird island.

elevation (left). With views towards the mainland descend onto the outer eastern side of Skrova. The elongated island of Nautøya lies directly ahead which is a bird and nature reserve. The path continues in a variety of ways below the steeply rising rock walls of Høgskrova to the rocky bay of **Merrvika ❺** which is located in the southwest. Ascend a scree slope to the **col ❻** to once more meet the illuminated cross-country ski run.

A path runs westwards onto Stappen mountain, 144m, while, to the east, it climbs steeply up onto Høgskrova. However, follow the 'illuminated', broad and well-trodden path to the next **junction ❼** in order to ascend the chain-protected path from here up to the highest elevation. On the broad plateau just before the summit you come past the distinctive Skrova radio mast. From the top of **Høgskrova ❽** you are rewarded with an impressive 360 degree panorama across the whole of the Vestfjorden with a view of the Lofoten chain of peaks and the mainland.

Descend the same way and follow the cross-country ski run as far as the gravel path, then finally continue along the surfaced road back to reach the **Heimskrova ❶** ferry dock.

↗ 800m | ↘ 800m | 7.9km

4.00 hrs

Suolovarri (Rundfjellet), 803m — 38

The island mountain

Suolovarri means in the Sami language 'island mountain'. Its expansive form towers up in the middle of Austvågøya surrounded by glacial lakes and boggy areas, with ascents from all directions and alpine terrain. It offers the determined walker a beautiful walk and a rewarding, fantastic 360 degree panorama.

Starting point: Storvassbotnen, parking, 38m. From the E 10 in Vestpollen turn off to Sandsletta and follow the Fv 7638 for about 5km. On the left hand side of the road there's a large boulder, and after that a sharp right hand bend with parking places on the left. From the Sandsletta campsite you will find parking after 4.5km on the right on a left hand bend.
Grade: you need to be very surefooted over the stony terrain; the path is difficult to find in places, especially in the alpine region from 500m upwards, and loses its way across scree slopes. There are large snowfields lasting into July on the northern and eastern slopes.
Infrastructure: campsite and restaurant in Sandsletta. Accommodation, café and supermarket in Laukvik. Accommodation, campsite, restaurants, supermarkets and petrol stations in Svolvær.
Alternative: from Vaterfjorden see p. 149.
Remarks: the path waymarked on the hiking map from the Botvatnet and Isvatnet lakes leads mainly over ground with no paths and should not be used on account of the delicate vegetation.
Map: Vågan.

View across the Vestfjorden with Stormolla and Litlmolla.

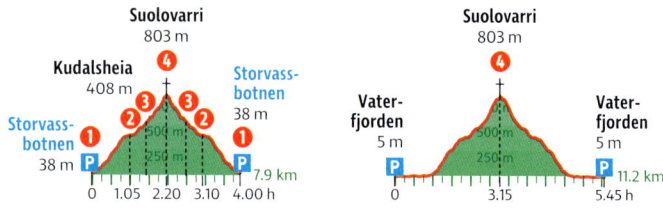

From the parking bay at the **Storvassbotnen** ❶ a well-trodden path runs southeastwards across an extensive boggy area with some trees. Ascend a broad ridge with partially slippery and damp rock steps on to **Kudalsheia** ❷. The orientation and route finding gets more difficult from here as it's now rocky underfoot and there's only the occasional cairn. After a depression you follow the broad ridge as far as a scree basin which you then cross over. Ascend the slope over broken rocks and then continue gently uphill over the continuously stony terrain. At last, from here, you can enjoy your first view of the **Vestfjorden** ❸.

From this point you need to head towards the mountain ridge on your right hand side. An unclear path now leads from the eastern side up onto this ridge and then runs along the ridge towards the summit ridge from where you will already be able to see the summit tower. You finally overcome the last scree slope lying ahead to reach the ridge which leads up to the 803m high summit of **Suolovarri** ❹. You look across the centre of Austvågøya, an alpine glacial landscape with patches of snow lasting into summer. Looking northeastwards you can see the highest mountains of the Lofoten – Higravtindan, Geitgallien (Walk 40) and Rulten – while in the south you can look as far across as the Norwegian mainland. In good

View from Suolovarri across Austvågøya.

weather even the furthest foothills of the Lofoten are visible in the west. Towards the northwest there are views across the lakes, fjords, bays and islands between Sandsletta and Laukvik.

For your return, we recommend the same path back down to the **Storvassbotnen** ❶.

Alternative: ascent from Vaterfjorden (5.45 hrs, 880 vertical metres, a 'black' walk; unclear path at times; the topography makes it easy for you to find your bearings)

About 4.5km north of Svolvær airport the E 10 leads across a bridge over the estuary of the **Vaterfjordpollen** (small parking place). A path runs along the north side of the pollen. Close to the power line which runs from the northeast to the southwest cross over Hellskarelva stream (an alternative crossing can be made at the estuary into the Vaterfjordpollen). Several muddy areas follow on after that (difficult route finding) and then the path leads up a wooded mountain slope. You continue to ascend northwestwards up this mountain ridge and then finally turn west and you can now see **Suolovarri** as you head towards the southern end of its summit ridge. There might still be some large snowfields to walk across here which can remain at altitudes of 500m and upwards right into July. From the southeast you now ascend the ridge onto the **summit** ❹.

Return the same way to Vaterfjorden.

39 Matmora, 788m

↗ 910m | ↘ 910m | 9.6km
4.30 hrs

'Mother of nourishment'

The crossing of Matmora – the name means 'mother of nourishment' – is a popular day's walk on the north side of Austvågøya which leads through varied mountain scenery which is different to any other landscape you will come across on a Lofoten walk: light forests, a lovely valley with a lake, alpine terrain, soft heathland, a descent over a long mountain ridge with views of the midnight sun (provided you are walking at night, of course) and at the end a pebbly beach on the Norwegian Sea. And along the way you come past bushes of blueberries, cranberries and cloudberrries, and mushrooms too. You will be able to watch ptarmigan on the lush areas of pastureland on the Gjersvollheia and from there have a wonderful view of the shimmering turquoise-blue water and the white sand banks of the Grunnførfjorden. At the end of the walk you can spend some time watching sea eagles near to the beach.

Starting point: car park on the Nordpollen of the Vatnfjorden on the FV 7638, 19m. A gravel path turns off sharp right 3km north of Sandsletta.
End point: walkers' car park near Delp. Return (6km) best made by bike.

Grade: long, moderately difficult walk on clearly visible and marked path (red waymarkers, cairns, signposts). There are scree slopes and rocky sections to overcome, some exposed sections on the descent.
Infrastructure: campsite and restaurant in Sandsletta. Accommodation, café and supermarket in Laukvik. Accommodation, camping, restaurants, supermarkets and petrol stations in Svolvær.
Alternatives: short walks are the ascent from the car park on the Nordpollen ❶ to Rangeldalen, 180m (30 mins to the lake, a 'blue' walk) as well as the ascent from the walkers' car park near Delp ❾ which takes you to the summits of Delpen, 374m, and Gjersvollheia, 424m (1 hr to the heia, 'red').
Tips: a good vantage point for watching the midnight sun is from the coast between Laukvik and Delp. In Laukvik, there is a small coffee roasting house called Keans Beans and in Straumnes, you can visit the Polarlightcenter.
Map: Vågan.

Blålyngen, 492m, on the Vatnfjorden.

Descent from Matmora across the heathland.

From the car park on the **Nordpollen** ❶ of the Vatnfjorden follow the roadway for a few metres to the south until a narrow footpath turns off to the left (sign for Ragnhilddalen). You are now walking along an old mule path that winds its way round many bends uphill. You are rewarded with wonderful views after only the first few bends.

After 20 minutes having already reached a height of 180m you arrive at the entrance into the **Rangeldalen** ❷. Foundation walls and ruins, constructed paths and holes in the southern hillside of Matmora are evidence of the mining activity that took place at the start of the 20th century. They expected to discover rich iron ore deposits, but their hopes were dashed after only a few years as the yield was simply too low.

After a short section through the shrubby birch trees and grassy areas the path forks. Take the right hand fork (tree with a wooden sign). At the following junction take the left hand foot path which continues straight ahead to Matmora (wooden sign), but it's worth making a detour to the right to **Rangeldalsvatnet** lake (5 minutes) to find a lovely spot where you can cool off with a swim on hot days.

The main path now gets quite a bit muddier and you come through a light birchwood with wonderful old trees that are bent double by the wind and

the weight of snow. Unfortunately there are very clear traces here of the devastation caused by moth invasions over the last few years. At the **end of the valley** ❸, the path swings northwards. Shortly after you start your climb through a scree field, you will pass the beginning of the Steindalen hanging valley. Keep left here to circumvent the scree field that lies ahead of you. Ignore the paths cutting across the scree field and take the path that runs alongside. From here, a small path goes up steeply. At the upper end of the scree field, change over to the path that climbs up to your right.

Continue to ascend steeply all the way up to a small col at an altitude of 750m. You are greeted with a magnificent view north where the turquoise-blue Grunnførfjorden lies shimmering ahead. It's now only 5 minutes across a scree slope and an area of boulders to reach the summit of **Matmora** ❹ where you are rewarded with a breathtaking 360 degree panorama.

From here you can get an impression of the path further along the edge of the ridge down to Gjersvollheia hill. The path always keeps left just below the ridge and you descend leisurely meadowed slopes with a few rocky sections. The descent is a bit steeper down to **Storskardet col** ❺ – be very careful if it's wet. (Walkers who started out from Delp should take special care here: the well-trodden path that leads to the right is the wrong one. The correct path ascends here on the left, on the eastern side!)

On the intermediary incline after the col there are two paths: one of them leads straight on steeply uphill and brings you onto the **529m high hill** ❻. But if you want to save yourself a few vertical metres, cross the hillside on

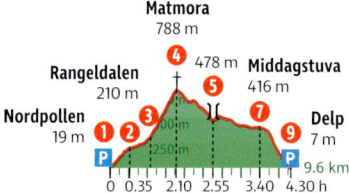

its eastern side. 10 minutes later descend to the large Gjersvollheia plateau which is a sheep pasture in summer and also ptarmigan territory. Numerous paths leads across the dense cushion-like tufts of heather. The shortest path runs along the western edge, but take the more picturesque path on the eastern side directly above the Grunnførfjorden. Here, you reach a big stone tower on the **Middagstuva** ❼, which is a popular tour destination. Your efforts will be rewarded with a magnficient view of the fjord and across the Norwegian Sea. After a good 400m, you reach the northernmost tip of Gjersvollheia, the **Delpen** ❽. Here, the path descends steeply through a birchwood down to the coast and the walkers' car park near the settlement of **Delp** ❾ on the Fv 7638.

To leave a bike before the walk would be a practical way of returning to your starting point at **Nordpollen** ❶, otherwise walk the 6km along the surfaced road or hitch hike.

High above the Grunnførfjorden.

↗ 1180m | ↘ 1180m | 8.4km

40 Geitgallien, 1085m

5.00 hrs

On the highest roof of the Lofoten

The second highest mountain of the Lofoten greets you with a breathtaking panorama and distant views across the elongated chain of the Lofoten islands. The alpine mountain terrain begins from an altitude of 500m above sea level. The path leads steeply uphill and at times in a direct climb to the summit.

Starting point: Liland, former shop, 5m. In Laupstad (about 22km northeast of Svolvær) on the E 10 follow the sign for Liland and the shop is on the left hand side after 900m.

Grade: for experienced alpine walkers. Surefootedness and route finding abilities over rough ground absolutely essential. Occasional sections of easy climbing. From 500m upwards there's hardly a visible path, or even no path at all, and the cairns marking the way are sparse. Largish areas of scree and gravel are crossed (danger of slipping here). Due to the location there are still large snowfields present here right into summer (where you might even need crampons). Good weather is a must for this walk.

Infrastructure: camping and restaurant in Sandsletta. Accommodation, camping, restaurants, supermarkets and petrol stations in Svolvær.

Map: Vågan.

As far as the eye can see.

An ascending roadway begins next to the former shop in **Liland** 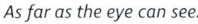 behind a gate which is, at the same time, the entrance to the illuminated cross country ski run (lysløypa). Follow the right hand ski run through a relatively dense and bushy birchwood into the Lilandsdalen. A green letter box on

The highest mountains of the Lofoten – Higravtindan and Geitgallien, with Sildpollen in front.

a pylon indicates the turning point of the **ski run** ❷. A narrow path now continues to the east towards a broad rock ledge over which the Skinelva stream tumbles down in a waterfall. The path winds its way past this steep section up the northern side of the valley. Afterwards keep on the left hand side of the valley. The at times dense vegetation thins out and the path becomes more stony. Ascend several steps to reach a **height of 550m** ❸. From here orientate yourself southeastwards towards a conspicuous rocky promontory. Cross the valley at the foot of this promontory and ascend the gully that follows to the east. You now cross areas of scree and snow in a valley running southeastwards which is bordered on its right hand side by jagged rock towers.

You reach a small **col** ❹ and a cirque opens up before you. On the right you can see a gully that leads steeply down into the Kvanndalen and further on to the Austpollen – a popular stretch for extreme skiers – while on the opposite side is located the pointed peak of Geitgallien. Cross over the snowfield in the cirque and then ascend the steep and slippery scree slope on the opposite side of the valley basin. From here you then make your way through the seemingly indomitable rocky summit area (a few cairns are a help with the route finding) to reach the large summit plateau of **Geitgallien** ❺. Return the same way to **Liland** ❶.

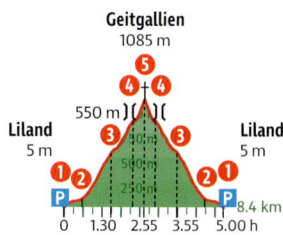

TOP 41 — **Keiservarden, 384m**

↗ 390m | ↘ 390m | 5.3km
1.45 hrs

A small peak with one of the loveliest panoramas

Kaiser Wilhelm II can be described as the initiator of Lofoten and Norwegian tourism. He walked up to this fantastic viewpoint above Raftsundet on one of his many visits to Norway on 19 July 1899. He built a cairn (varden) on the top of Digermulkollen and so the summit has been called Keiservarden ever since. The Lofoteners make use of this fact as an opportunity to organise, every year in July since 1989, the 'Keisermarsjen' – a jolly and colourful walkers' festival for the whole family.

The emperor's view across the Raftsundet.

Starting point: between Digermulen and Valen, 5m. From the E 10 east of the Raftsundet bridge take the turning onto the Fv 7630 and follow this road for 21km to Digermulen. After Digermulen a large gravel square for parking can be found a short way before the village name sign for Valen on the right hand side of the road.
Grade: obvious path, signposted and waymarked with wooden posts and plastic bands.
Infrastructure: accommodation, food shop and café as well as a self-service petrol pump in Digermulen.
Alternative: Snøtinden, 637 m (from Keiservarden 2.30 hrs, 470 vertical metres in ascent and descent, a 'red' walk): from Keiservarden a tiny path leads northeastwards to Digermulvatnet lake (barbecue site). After the lake the path is obvious, but then it loses itself on the ascent up the hillside of Snøtinden; pathless terrain to the summit.
Tips: the German painter Christian-Ivar Hammerbeck exhibits his work in a small gallery (about 2km from the centre of the village in the district of Valen, following the signs for the Atelier Trollfjord).
An interesting detour to a small bay for a swim and along the coast brings you to Årsteinen.
Regular ferries leave from Digermulen to the island of Stormolla.
Map: Vågan.

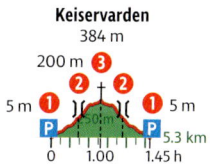
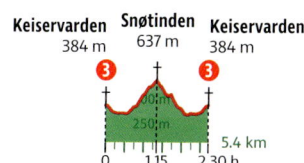

Photo above: Raftsundet bridge.
Left: the Trolltindan massif on Raftsundet.

Walk from the **car park** ❶ a few steps back towards Digermulen. From here a wooden sign indicates the start of the footpath on the opposite side of the road. Ascend through a forest of birch trees and conifers into a valley. The path is well-trodden and occasionally wet. Just before the going gets steeper uphill, the path turns left. At an altitude of 200m you reach a **col** ❷ where you meet a path that leads down to the left to Digermulen. Continue along the main path. The birch trees begin to thin out increasingly and from about a height of 280m the terrain is dominated by rocky hillocks and dense cushions of heather. In the area of the degraded summit plateau, there are several paths. Take the left hand one which brings you to a cairn on the edge of the rock and from here you can look down to Digermulen. After another 400m we reach the summit of the Digermulkollen massif – the **Keiservarden** ❸ where two cairns and memorial plaques testify to the German emperor's visit.

From here on the top you can experience a unique and beautiful panorama. If you are there between 16.00 and 18.00 you will see the Hurtigruten ships as they sail through the Raftsundet.

Take the same path back down to the **car park** ❶.

↗ 540m | ↘ 540m | 7.7km

42 The Dronningstien on Årsteinen (Stortinden), 530m

2.30 hrs

Southernmost peak of Hinnøya

On the southernmost spur of Norway's largest island of Hinnøya, near Digermulen, lies the small peninsula of Årsteinen with its white sandy beaches and the Stortinden massif. The path to the summit is a varied walk for the whole family and runs along an historic path. There's a plaque commemorating an ascent of Stortinden in 2016 and in 2017 by Queen Sonja of Norway who has been coming to Northern Norway to go walking for many years. Since then the path from Pundslett and Årstein to the summit has been known as the Dronningstien (Queen's Path). The first Dronningvarden in Norway has been standing on the summit since 2016.

Starting point: Årstein (south of Digermulen), car park, 6m. After Digermulen take the turning (Fv 7632) towards Pundsletta and Årstein. Drive 7.3km to Årstein, turn right at a little red letter box house and follow the signposts for the car park.
Grade: obvious and well-trodden path; there are some signposts, but no waymarkers.
Infrastructure: accommodation, small food shop and café as well as self-service petrol pump in Digermulen.
Tip: make a visit to the Atelier Trollfjord in Valen.
Map: Vågan.

Norway's first Dronningvarden, placed by Queen Sonja.

Newly signposted.

You can see the summit of Stortinden directly from the car park in **Årstein** ❶. Follow the roadway past the houses to the signposts that indicate the path up to Årsteinskaret col, Stortinden and Pundslett. You drove through the latter village on your way from Digermulen to Årsteinen. From the signposts your path leads

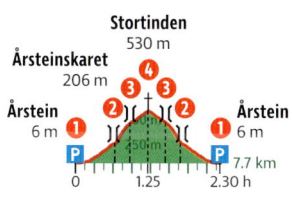

across a meadow towards a little birchwood and in the direction of the col which you climb up to. The path runs along the old road that used to link Årsteinen and Pundslett.

On the **Årsteinskaret col** ❷ turn left and walk uphill. During the ascent you have a beautiful view of Pundslettvatnet. You can soon see the summit ridge ahead that takes you to your destination. But first, you reach a flat **col** ❸ from where you can take a short detour of 500m to Litjeårsteintinden.

In order to reach the summit of Stortinden turn left and walk up along the mountain ridge. After 900m, you reach the Dronningvarden on **Stortinden** ❹. From here you are rewarded with a view of the many islands in the Svællingsflaket nature conservation aea in the east and southeast of Årsteinen, and over as far as the Norwegian mainland. Look west to see Austvågøya and Stormolla, Litlmolla and Skrova.

Return the same way to **Årstein** ❶.

Walking on the Vesterålen

In contrast to the elongated Lofoten, the Vesterålen islands form a much more compact group of islands, which extends towards its northernmost tip at a line of latitude just over 69 degrees north. The archipelago is characterised by a multitude of fjords and straits. The large main islands are the heavily fragmented Langøya (Vesterålen's largest island), Andøya, Hadseløya and part of the islands of Austvågøya and Hinnøya. There are also innumerable smaller islands and skerries. The longest waterway of the Vesterålen is the Sortlandsundet which separates the islands of Langøya and Hinnøya and constitutes an important traffic route. The fishing industry plays the biggest economic role here too, followed by agriculture. Tourism is less developed in the Vesterålen.

Like the Lofoten, Vesterålen also consists of interesting mountain ranges for the walker, some with alpine character, and sections of coastline exposed to the Norwegian Sea, beautiful sandy beaches and peatland which cover large parts of the islands.

On the Sortlandsundet.

The cradle of the Hurtigruten lies on the Vesterålen.

Municipality of Hadsel: the cradle of the Hurtigruten

The municipality of Hadsel joins the Lofoten to the north. Like Vågan, it stretches across several different islands and parts of islands: Hadseløya, the southernmost part of the eastern side of Langøya, the northern part of Austvågøya, and the southwestern part of Hinnøya. The Hadselfjorden and Sortlandsundet waterways separate the individual parts of the municipality from each other. Hadseløya is connected to the island of Langøya by an architecturally perfect bridge where it's interesting to watch the Hurtigruten ships sailing through. There are ferry services to Hinnøya and Austvågøya.

Near the coast, large parts of the municipality are dominated by farming, but the fishing industry plays the main role. The majority of the 8000 inhabitants live in Melbu and Stokmarknes on Hadseløya. Stokmarknes is considered to be the birthplace of the Hurtigruten and it was here that the Vesteraalens Dampsskibsselskab shipping company was founded which, from 1893 onwards, operated the Hurtigruten line. Their story is documented in the museum in the Hurtigruten Hus which is well worth a visit. There are some strenuous walks amidst a wonderful landscape awaiting the walker – from the unique alpine setting of the Trollfjordhytta across the lofty heights of Lamlitinden to the summit of Møysalen, the highest mountain of both the archipelagos (Walks 43 to 47).

Alternating light and shade patterns at every turn.

Municipality of Sortland: in the heart of Vesterålen

The main settlement areas of Sortland municipality (10,000 inhabitants) which consists of parts of the islands of Langøya and Hinnøya, are confined to the coastal areas along the protected Sortlandsundet which lies between the two islands, the northern side of the climatically favoured Sigerfjorden and the northern foothills of the Eidsfjorden. The economic centre, the largest shopping centre and the largest town in the municipality and the whole of Vesterålen is Sortland. Its modern history began in 1370 with the construction of a church and an associated estate. In 1900 only 253 people lived in this place that had grown into a trading and business centre, but today there are more than 5000 inhabitants. Witnesses to former times, such as the old bell tower from the 15th century and the old Sortland guesthouse are still to be found in the centre. An idea of modern times is the 'blue city' project adopted as an art project by the city which is the reason why blue is the dominant colour in the centre of Sortland. The Norwegian Coast Guard which has its headquarters here and its ships can be seen in the port. At the narrowest point of the Sortlandsundet, the 948m long Sortlandbrua bridge has been connecting the islands of Hinnøya and Langøya since 1975.

Like all the islands of the Vesterålen, the districts belonging to Sortland are dominated by mountain ranges of various heights and levels of difficulty. In this guide book we decided to describe the walks to Skata (Walk 51), Stortinden (Walk 50) and the varied route to Snytindhytta (Walk 49) in the alpine heart of Hinnøya. Our multi-day hike (Walk 48) through the alpine heart of Hinnøya starts from the E 10 on the Ingelsfjordeidet in the municipality of Lødingen (which no longer lies on the Vesterålen) and ends in the municipality of Sortland on the Fv 822.

Municipality of Bø – where the world 'ends'

The smallest municipality (2600 inhabitants) located in the southwest of Vesterålen is characterised by its extreme remoteness. It might be located on Langøya, but just on the southwestern part of the severely fragmented island. The one and only land route has been going through the Ryggedals tunnel since 1980 when it replaced the previously required ferries. You need to allow more than one hour for the 57km drive along the Fv 820 from Sortland to Straume.

The area of the municipality consists of many larger and smaller peninsulas which at times are only connected with one another over narrow land bridges and surrounded by countless really small islands and skerries. The Eidsfjorden lies in the east which cuts deep into Langøya island, otherwise the coast of Bø is largely exposed to the Norwegian Sea.

Compared to the other municipalities, everything here is even more contemplative and quiet, but all the more intense – an ideal hiking area with both easy and intermediate walks (Walks 52 to 56). Stone Age tombs, billion year old rock formations, bird cliffs, bogs and mountains, fjords, skerries and islands are your companions. And, of course, the Norwegian Sea whose strength and beauty is probably felt nowhere more intensely than in Hovden, the 'end of the world'.

Killi Olsen's Mannen fra havet sculpture in Vinjesjøen (municipality of Bø).

Municipality of Øksnes: diverse landscape at the vastness of the Norwegian Sea

The name Øksnes comes from the parish of the same name on the island of Skogsøya which was once the centre of the old community. Today the northwestern part of Langøya Island and a number of smaller inhabited islands belong to the municipality (4500 inhabitants) whose community centre is Myre. The main industries are fishing and agriculture. With the resurgence of the fishing village of Nyksund, at least for tourists, the oldest surviving church of Vesterålen in Langenes, whale watching tours and the scenic and historic islands of Vestbygda and Skogsøya, the municipality of Øksnes has much to offer its visitors. The Dronningruta walk which we describe in this guide  (Walk 58) was declared the most beautiful hike in Norway in 2012, while from Nonskollen (Walk 57) you can enjoy a wonderful view across the different forms of natural landscapes that are prevalent in this area.

Municipality of Andøy: between bogs, research centres and whale watching

The municipality Andøy (just under 5000 inhabitants) can also boast a wide variety of attractions. The border between the municipalities of Sortland and Andøy runs along the Forfjorden, so that not only Andøya island of the same name, but also the northwestern tip of Hinnøya island both belong to the municipality. South of the Forfjorden you can marvel at some of Scandinavia's oldest Scots pines.

The very shallow Risøysundet which separates the two islands can be crossed over the impressive Andøybrua bridge. In addition to the steeply towering peaks and over 300 lakes, Andøya consists predominantly of large boggy areas which are barely 10 to 20m above sea level. Andmyran bog with its 100km^2 is the largest continuous area of bogs in Norway. In the northwest of Andøya, surrounded by the oldest terminal moraine and one of the most beautiful and longest sandy beaches in Norway, is the small town of Bleik. Some of the walks described by us in Walk 59 start from this point.

The agricultural areas of the Vesterålen nestle up to the fjords.

The bird island of Bleiksøya lies here just off the coast. At the northern tip of the island is Andenes, Norway's northwesternmost point – former military base and space research centre. Today you can take tours to watch sperm whales at the spot from where the whalers used to set off. Apart from this, Andenes is an ideal place to observe both the midnight sun and the polar lights.

The Andøya Space Centre is dedicated to atmospheric research and for this purpose, and others, research rockets are launched south of Andenes. The last of our walks also explores the region around the Alomar Observatory (Walk 60).

For an overall impression of Andøya it's worth taking a trip along the Andfjorden to explore its inner side and on the Norwegian Sea for views of its outer side. On the Fv 82 you pass the remnants of a 1800 year old ring fortress in Åse and in Dverberg you can visit a small soap manufacturer with a café. While driving along the Fv 82 beside the large bogs and peat-digging areas in Kvalnesmyran, the outer coastal road (Fv 7702 and Fv 7698) offers a variety of rugged coastlines, bogs and mountain ranges. In Nøss you can make an interesting visit to the gallery of the same name and in Bø, stop at the Nordtun Gård farm dairy. Burial mounds and the remains of a Stone Age settlement (Sletten-Bakken) can be found south of Bø.

↗ 470m | ↘ 470m | 5.6km
3.00 hrs

43 Trollfjordhytta, 405m

High above the Trollfjorden in the alpine heart of Austvågøya

The Trollfjorden is the most famous fjord north of the polar circle. It branches off from the Raftsundet and is just 2.5km long. At its narrowest point it measures only 100m and is towered over by high rock walls. The depth of the fjord is 72m. The fjord was made famous by the Trollfjord battle: on March 6, 1890, there was a fight between hundreds of traditional Lofoten fishermen with their Nordland boats and four modern steamboats which had closed off the entrance to the fjord and were trying to catch the herring with drainage nets. This battle was memorably commemorated in the national literature by Johan Bojer in the 'Den siste Viking' ('The Last of the Vikings') and in the painting 'Trollfjordslaget' by Gunar Berg. The painting hangs in the town hall of Svolvær. The Trollfjorden has been a tourist attraction for over 100 years. Today, Hurtigruten ships sail into the fjord during the summer months. On March 30, 1987 an American A-10 Thunderbolt crashed at Isvasstinden, 940m, above the Trollfjorden. In memory of the pilot Robert D. Wallen, who lost his life, the summit is now also called Wallentind.

Starting point: boat mooring at the Trollfjorden hydroelectric power station, 3m. Access to the fjord is only possible by boat. From Svolvær there are daily boat trips in the summer months from here (information at the tourist office in Svolvaer, tel. +47 76070575, lofoten.info/no/Turistinformasjoner, or directly at the harbour in Svolvær). The boats don't dock regularly in the Trollfjorden so you have to arrange this with the ferry company as well as your pick-up time too.
Grade: waymarked footpath, in places muddy and scree-covered.
Infrastructure: Trollfjordhytta which is a self-catering mountain hut of the Vesterålen Turlag with a total of 20 spaces (information: vesteralen.dnt.no).
Alternatives: ascent of Blåskavltinden; for the description see p. 171.

MS Trollfjord at the entrance into the Trollfjorden.

Detour onto Isvasshaugen, see p. 170. There's an alternative start to this walk (4km) from the Austpollen across the Austpolldalen following the electricity power line. But this also requires a transfer by boat from the E 10 (about 5–6km north of Higrav) across the Sløverfjorden/Austpollen.

Tip: from Isvasshaugen you have a view down onto the Trollfjorden lying a long way below. The Hurtigruten boats heading southwards enter the Trollfjorden at around 17.00 and provide brilliant photo opportunities.

Remarks: the alternative from Holdøya along the Sløverfjord described in local walking guides is to be avoided at all costs due to the lack of paths, the intricate terrain and the length of the walk.

The ascent of the 940m high Wallentind (Isvasstinden) which is also described in local walking guides is only accessible to walkers over rough ground up to a height of 587m and after that involves proper climbing.

Maps: Vågan and Vesterålen – Hinnøya Sør.

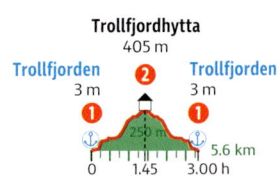

Fascinating reflections on the Isvatnet near to the Trollfjordhytta.

Start at the hydroelectric power station in the **Trollfjorden** ❶, walk left around the building and follow the penstock pipes. After a quarter of an hour the path brings you westwards along beside a small stream through a very boggy side valley. Then follows a steep and stony incline between dense ferns on the northwest slope of a valley shelf. Afterwards cross some sections of scree and ascend a last incline on your left hand side. Surrounded by up to 1000m high mountains you now look down into a large valley basin and be amazed at the alpine landscape at just 400m in altitude. It's only a short walk over undulating, rocky ground to the **Trollfjordhytta** ❷ where the huts are located by a small bay on Isvatnet lake.

Isvasshaugen, 504m (100 vertical metres), rises up to the east of the moutain huts from where you can walk up to the summit by taking a detour of 20 minutes along a tiny track. From the top here you have a great view of the Trollfjorden way down below.

Return the same way to the **Trollfjorden** ❶.

Alternative: Blåskavltinden, 975m (4.00 hrs, 730 vertical metres, a 'black' walk; this path makes high demands on surefootedness, requires a lack of vertigo, route finding across rough ground, and also experience in alpine terrain)

At first follow the waymarked footpath from the old **Trollfjordhytta** ❷ in the direction of Austpollen as far as the Austpollskaret col, 500m. From then onwards you continue westwards across rough ground as far as a short intermediary descent. A long incline then follows (also without paths) up to the prominent col on the left below Blåskavltinden. From here it's a very steep climb up the meadowed slope to the summit plateau.
Return the same way to the **Trollfjordhytta** ❷.

View from Isvasshaugen into the Trollfjorden.

↗ 970m | ↘ 970m | 11.4km
5.30 hrs

44 Strøna, 906m

On the north side of Austvågøya

Situated in the northern part of Austvågøya and belonging to the Vesterålen municipality of Hadsel, Strøna appears rather unremarkable. Its height is, however, considerable. And viewed from Hadseløya it rises up like a pyramid with steep flanks and a mighty summit structure above the Hadselfjorden.

Starting point: Strønstad, car park before the Tresmia wood carving workshop, 3m, signposted from the Fv 7638, 3.5km west of Fiskebøl.

Grade: this is at first an easy walk, but then becomes more demanding from the col ❸ and is exposed in places; surefootedness and a lack of vertigo absolutely essential, easy climbing in the summit area, waymarked footpath (plastic waymarkers on trees, cairns), difficult route finding from 600m upwards.
Infrastructure: camping and restaurant in Sandsletta. Accommodation, café and supermarket in Laukvik. Accommodation, restaurants, supermarkets and petrol stations in Svolvær and Melbu.
Maps: Vågan and Vesterålen – Hinnøya Sør.

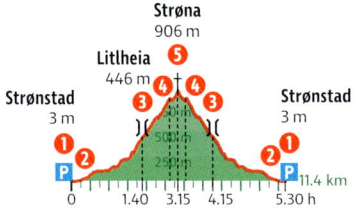

The damp air rising from the sea frequently accumulates on Stona.

From the car park in **Strønstad** ❶ walk back to the tarmac road and turn left. After about 75m a roadway turns off to the south (right) in the direction of the Strøndalen and brings you to some houses. Walk on the left past a red-painted barn and then leave the roadway after a good 100m. A sign indicates the **turn-off** ❷.

The path leads as far as the Dalsvatnet lake through a little muddy, light birchwood. After the lake it continues uphill into the Litldalen. The shallow, grass-covered Litldalen ends in a valley basin. You are surrounded by mountains, Sellåterfjellet and Nonsfjellet in the west and Middagsfjellet in the south while the western flank of Strøna rises up in the northeast, but you can't see its summit yet.

There's a stony path ahead winding its way up the steep hillside to **Litlheia col** ❸. From the col you can look down into the neighbouring Fiskebøldalen and across the valley to Trolldalstinden, 833m, and Brettvikstindan, 836m.

Follow the obvious and well-worn path along the ridge towards the summit of Strøna. At 600m and above you have to find your way between the very few cairns up the eastern flank and not let yourself be led astray by the many sheep tracks that circle the hillside. After your ascent up the flank you reach the top of a large **elevation** ❹. You are almost there: the rocky summit is already towering ahead of you. After a short descent, the path finally goes up the western side of the mountain. Some easy scrambling takes you to the summit of **Strøna** ❺.

Return the same way to the **starting point** ❶.

The tower-like summit is still not visible from here.

↗ 880m | ↘ 880m | 10.5km
5.30 hrs

45 Lamlitinden, 657m

Hadseløya's highest mountain

You're in the right place here if you like an airy feel to your walks. This path runs high above the outer edge of Hadseløya with views of Austvågøya in the south, Hinnøya in the east and Langøya in the north. The open sea and the offshore skerries of Hadseløya lie in the west.

Starting point: Ånnstad, 8m. About 6km northwest of Melbu, a gravel path branches off on the right after the Fv 7634 crosses a small stream. You can either park along the road or continue on the gravel path for 500m for more parking.
Grade: unmarked, in places with no paths, exposed, ridge walk with airy sections.
Infrastructure: accommodation, restaurants, supermarkets and petrol stations in Melbu and Stokmarknes.
Alternatives: 1. Descent from Lamlitinden to Taskaret col and from there along beside the lakes to Teigan: on the descent to the lakes there are large sections without paths, in particular a steep descent of 200 vertical metres above Øvrevatnet lake (from Lamlitinden 4.4km, 680m of descent, 1.50 hrs); a bike or a second car is needed in order to return to your starting point.
2. Descent from Lamlitinden to Taskaret col and continue west here below Tanipa across the steep slope in the direction of Finnsæterkollen. Be careful here – this section is very exposed and you could easily fall. The rest of the descent is described in Walk 46; take a look at the map there too.
Tips: the small peninsula Taneset can be found north of the starting point.

Lamlitinden packs a punch – an exhilarating experience for vertigo free walkers.

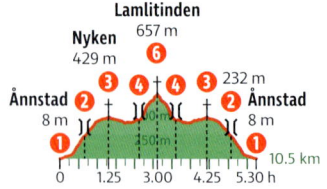

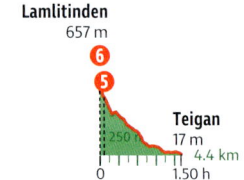

It has a small beach where you can take a stroll or enjoy a swim. If you drive further on you will come to the inconspicuous sign on the left hand side to the Uværshula which is a simple shelter for use in bad weather. It lies amidst a rocky coastline and is a popular destination for daytrippers. You can drive the 42km all around the island of Hadseløya on the Fv 82 and FV 7634, but this would also be an ideal place for a bike ride.
Hurtigruten Museum in Stokmarknes, see Walk 46.
The Norwegian Fishing Industry Museum in Melbu is an interesting place to visit, and also the Vesterålen Museum (see Walk 46 for info).
On the road between Stokmarknes and Melbu you drive past Hadsel church that was built in 1824. It houses some old cultural objects (e.g. a Russian Messing chandelier from the 13th century) which have been preserved from the former building.
Map: Vesterålen – Hinnøya Sør.

Start the walk along a gravel path in **Ånnstad** ❶ that leads northeastwards into the broad Ånnstaddalen. After 5 minutes you pass a quarry/gravel pit and shortly after that, on the left hand side of the valley, you can see a clear, but unmarked path running up the hillside which you follow all the way up to **Storskardet col** ❷.
You meet a footpath that leads in an easterly direction along the broad ridge of Seterfjellet. However, turn west along this path and follow the bamboo stick waymarkers up to Pallheia plateau where **Nyken** ❸ stands on the western side with its clearly visible tower marking the highest

The coastline is dotted everywhere with small sandy beaches.

point. For those walkers with a good head for heights there's an optional continuation of the path as far as the prominent peak lying ahead, 412m. The path now continues northwards along the edge of the plateau and afterwards along a narrower ridge. Then it leads on the eastern side below the jagged rocky summit of Kråkhammartind, 444m, and Storlitinden, 475m, as far as a **col** ❹. From here continue steeply uphill across the grassy slope, at times with no paths, as far as the foremost summit of the ridge (Durmålstindan, 530m).

The path now becomes exposed along the ridge. After about 100m it changes onto the northwestern side and your gaze falls on the summit of Tanipa, 572m. Descend gently down the hillside meadow and after about 120m you are standing at an inconspicuous **crossing point** ❺ where the footpath continues downhill to a small mountain lake and Taskaret col. However, ascend the gully steeply uphill (no paths) and a very airy path on the ridge finally brings you to the summit of **Lamlitinden** ❻.
Return the same way to the **starting point** ❶.

↗ 430m | ↘ 430m | 5.1km

2.00 hrs

Finnsæterkollen, 439m | 46

A beautiful walk for the young and old

The ascent to Finnsæterkollen is an easy walk for the whole family on the southwest edge of Hadseløya island. It is also an ideal place to be walking during the time of the midnight sun. If you happen to go for a walk in stormy weather, you can find shelter in the Uværshula on the coast and watch the thundering waves crash on the beach while in warm weather, you can cool off with a swim at the small Taneset beach which offers picnic and barbecue facilities.

View from the summit of Tanipa, 572m.

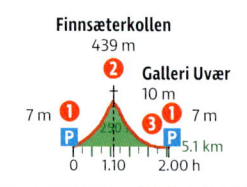

Starting point: parking bay on the Fv 7634, 7m. From the ferry dock in Melbu drive 13.1km in a westerly direction; from the Hurtigruten Museum in Stokmarknes 12.7km, also to the west. The small parking bay is situated on the left hand side (coming from Melbu), shortly before the Uvær gallery.

Grade: easy, comfortable unmarked path. Somewhat steeper on the way up to the summit.

Infrastructure: accommodation, restaurants, supermarkets and petrol stations in Melbu and Stokmarknes.

Tips: the Uværshula can be found just near the parking bay which is a simple shelter that can be used in bad weather conditions in the middle of a rocky coastal landscape. There's also the Uvær gallery and a small café nearby.

As you drive towards Melbu you will come to the small peninsula Taneset (Taen). Its pleasant small beach is an inviting spot for a stroll and a swim and there's the small climbing area of Trollskåla just next to it.

You can drive the 42km right round the island of Hadseløya on the Fv 82 and Fv 7634, also an ideal place for a bike ride. The birthplace of the Hurtigruten is considered to be on the Vesterålen and the interesting Hurtigruten Museum in Stokmarknes gives a fantastic insight into its history and is recommended for a visit. The old M/S Finnmarken is also open to visitors next to the museum. The Norwegian Fishing Industry Museum in Melbu, which experienced an industrial boom between 1890 and 1920, is an interesting place to visit, and also the Vesterålen Museum located on land belonging to the old Melbo estate is worth taking a look at.

On the road between Stokmarknes and Melbu you drive past Hadsel church, built in 1824. It houses some old cultural objects (e.g. a Russian Messing chandelier from the 13th century) preserved from the former building.

Map: Vesterålen – Hinnøya Sør.

Frequent companions along the way.

From the **parking bay** ❶ walk about 60m to the northeast along the road and then turn right onto a roadway where you are heading towards a group of houses. At the point where the roadway ends turn right onto a single track grassy path and walk past the houses. After passing a gate follow the left hand bend in the path and ascend to a broad ridge covered in heather. Turn to the right here and follow the path along the ridge continuously uphill as far as the summit of Finnsæterkollen. As you do so, on your left hand side there are views of the glacial landscape surrounding Teigvatnet, Jordvatnet and Øvrevatnet lakes.

Once you arrive on **Finnsæterkollen** ❷ you look down onto the coastline of Hadseløya and also across the Eidsfjorden onto the part of Langøya which belongs to the municipality of Bø, and the offshore islands of Gaukværøya and Litløya. You can see ahead the jagged summit of Tanipa. If you feel like it, you can continue towards Tanipa which is a bit more airy and takes you to an elevation of 513m.

Return at first down the same path. At the broad ridge however, continue straight on which brings you directly to the **Galleri Uvær** ❸ and from there along the road back to the **parking bay** ❶.

TOP 47

↗ 1650m | ↘ 1650m | 25.4km
10.30 hrs

Møysalen, 1262m

From sea level onto the highest peak of the Vesterålen

With its 51.2km², the Møysalen nasjonalpark is one of the smallest national parks in Norway. The protection of this park and that of the adjoining nature reserve stretches from wonderful fjords, unique in their own way in Norway (the Innerfjorden, Ingelsfjorden and Lonkanfjorden) across lush laurel forests high up into the alpine mountain scenery of Møysalen. The mountain gets its name from the two petrified 'troll maidens', Lille Møya and Store Møya (Møyene), the two distinctive peaks that stand to the south of Møysalen. The saddle-shaped Møysalen is often described as the roof of her room or as a saddle for her horse (both are 'sal' in Norwegian).

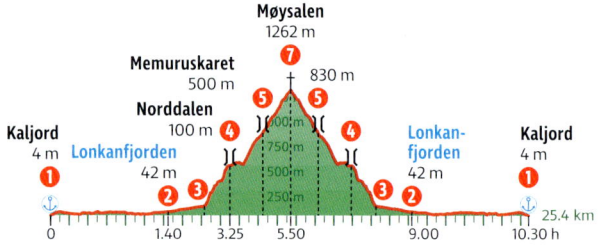

Starting point: Kaljord, ferry dock, 4m. Access along the Fv 822, or by ferry from Hanøy (about 2.6km northwest of Raftsundet bridge on the E 10) or by ferry from Stokmarknes (177nordland.no).
Grade: very long walk (25.4km), demanding alpine territory from 600m upwards with scree slopes, old snowfields lasting into summer, chain protection in places and in the summit area there's a glacier to be crossed (depending on the weather crampons and an axe might also be necessary). Stamina as well as a very good degree of sure-footedness and experience in alpine country are required for this walk.

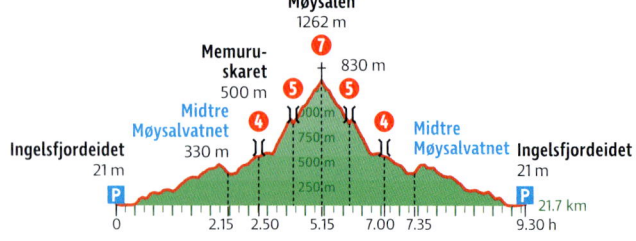

Infrastructure: national park campsite, cabins, small supermarket and café in the national park information centre in Hennes (northwest of Kaljord). There's also a small supermarket and petrol pump in Kaljord.

Alternatives: there are several alternative access points and/or ascent routes onto Møysalen. The most well-known and most frequently used path is, however, the main one described from Kaljord.

1. Approach from Ingelsfjordeidet (9.30 hrs, just under 22km there and back, 1900 vertical metres, a 'black' walk): from the car park in Ingelsfjordeidet through the Forkledalen valley as far as Midtre Møysalvatnet lake (see Walk 48 for the description). From there along a clear path waymarked with cairns as far as Memuruskaret col ❹. From here, see the description below.
2. Approach from the Snytindhytta for a multi-day walk (Walk 49). From there continue in the reverse direction of Walk 48.

Tip: you can join guided walks onto Møysalen from the national park centre. It is also possible to take a shuttle boat into the Lonkanfjorden and in this way shorten the walk. For more information, visit moeysalen.no.

Map: Vesterålen – Hinnøya Sør.

In the lovely Norddalen.

Above the ferry dock in **Kaljord** ❶ follow a gravel roadway leisurely uphill. After 10 minutes a sign indicates the footpath that turns off left. For the next few kilometres you are walking along a very varied path – through extremely muddy sections in a birchwood, along the steep coastline of a fjord, across former agriculturally used areas of meadow and past old foundation walls belonging to various farms. After 90 minutes you reach the old settlement of Gammelgården where you can take a break beside a burbling mountain stream. After that you pass a small rock ledge at which point you are approaching the end of the **Lonkanfjorden** ❷.

From here walk along an old cart track which was constructed for ore mining northeastwards into the Norddalen, the valley which is characterised by a wonderful boggy landscape. From the **end of the valley** ❸ continue along a steep and stony path up the rocky slopes of the head of the valley onto **Memuruskaret col** ❹. From the col there's a fantastic view into an extremely waterlogged valley. The alternative approaches come through this valley.

From Memuruskaret col you now continue in a northerly direction. Walk up a gentle slope and after a short intermediary descent into a valley with a stream (last opportunity for drinking water) it's now a steep climb to reach the Fonnisen glacier located in the large valley basin. The petrified troll maidens of Lille Møya and Store Møya tower above the glacier. Ascend

Above the Øvre Møysalvatnet.

At the Fonnisen glacier opposite Møysalen, Lille Møya and Store Møya.

the scree slope a short way in a northerly direction then, after that, follow the sparsely placed cairns at first westwards and then northwards for about 80 vertical metres onto a hill. Be very careful here not to attempt the steep and difficult scree slope that lies ahead. From the top of the hill you can enjoy a wonderful view of the Øvre Møysalvatnet lake. Descend northeastwards to the **col** ❺ which is located at an altitude of 830m.

From here follow the traces of a path on the left below the ridge, cross a scree slope and climb up 100 vertical metres through very rocky terrain (two places are protected with a chain) onto the **1000 metre plateau** ❻. The mighty butress of Møysalen looms up on the opposite side and you now head straight towards it. Walk around the steepest part on the right hand side up the stepped rocky terrain, again looking out for the occasional cairn. After overcoming the butress you still have to cross the Øverbreen glacier and negotiate a few more vertical metres over scree. To reach the glacier you must first clamber down the stepped rocky terrain for several metres. After many hours you are at last standing on the highest mountain of Vesterålen, **Møysalen** ❼, and are rewarded with the indescribably breathtaking 360 degree panorama.

Return along the same path to the **starting point** ❶.

↗ 2000m | ↘ 2000m | 27.2km

48 Multi-day walk through the Møysalen nasjonalpark

3 days

Into the Hinnøya alps

This wonderful and very varied walk is the only long distance hiking route of both archipelagos that is waymarked throughout. It begins virtually at sea level and leads through boggy landscapes right up into alpine territory at altitudes between 400 and 730m. On its way it crosses through the small Møysalen nasjonalpark and the adjoining nature reserves. We have deliberately not divided the walks into daily stages so that walkers can decide the destination for themselves on each day and places where they are going to stay overnight. For those wanting to extend the walk even further there's an optional ascent offered here onto Møysalen (Walk 47) which can be included into this multi-day trip.

Starting point: car park on the Ingelsfjordeidet, 21m, on the E 10; 17.6km southwest of the Gullesfjordbottn roundabout.
End point: car park on the Fv 822 at the junction with the Rv 85, shortly before or after the Sigerfjord tunnel, 75m. The best way to return to your starting point is to hitch a lift (bus connections are complicated and taxis very expensive).
Grade: predominantly well-marked and signposted footpath. Long sections through boggy terrain, walking across water courses (taking trekking sandals or gym shoes for wading across are a good idea). In the alpine areas the path is for the most part stony and sometimes covered in scree. Surefootedness and experience in alpine country are absolutely essential. If you choose to include in the trip the ascent of the 'black' no. 47 walk onto Møysalen, then extra stamina is needed as well as surefootedness and experience in high alpine terrain. Please read carefully the grade description and directions for Walk 47!
Infrastructure: there are no places to eat along the way, so you have to take all necessary provisions with you (see 'Remarks').
There are places to put up a tent by the Midtre Møysalvatnet, Tverrelvvatnan, Nedre Møysalvatnet, Langvatnet lakes and along the Småtindane. The Snytindhytta is an open, unstaffed mountain hut of the Vesterålen Turlag (VT) with 22 spaces. The mountain hut can also be used without an overnight stay in which case you pay a fee for the day. Money is placed in an envelope, but can also be transferred. It's possible to make reservations at the Vesterålen Turlag (VT), vesteralen.dnt.no.

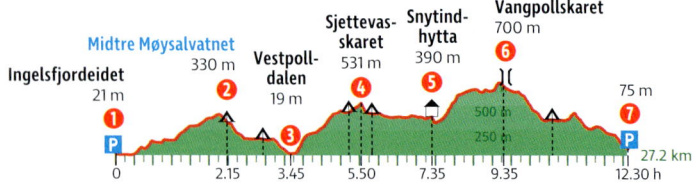

On the Midtre Møysalvatnet.

Alternatives: there are various alternative routes and extensions of the path along the way; see below for the description.

Remarks: the kilometre details in the walk description and profile relate to the GPS coordinates. Sometimes you will find that these differ from the details on signposts.

Provisions: the amount of food depends on how long you plan to spend on the walk and, of course, individual tastes. Practical ideas for hot meals might be a selection of your own prepared dried foods or industrially produced and freeze-dried foods which can be cooked directly in the packet. Otherwise a combination of muesli, powdered milk, nourishment bars, nut assortments, chocolate and bread. It makes sense to also include at least one reserve meal. There is plenty of water available along the way.

Equipment: wind-resistent tent, a three-season sleeping bag (be aware that temperatures can drop below 0 °C in the autumn), rucksack including a rain cover, sturdy waterproof mountain walking boots, gym shoes or trekking sandals for walking through boggy areas and streams/water courses, a set of (warm) clothes to change into, warm (wool) underwear, rain and wind proof jacket and trousers, warm jacket (down/synthetic fibre), cap and/or headscarf, gloves, warm socks, map, possibly a GPS device, stove and cooking utensils, water bottle, food.

Season: late summer and autumn are the best seasons. Admittedly the days are not so long, but there is hardly any danger of snowfields. Also there can be less water in the boggy sections of the walk, although temperatures are palpably cooler.

Map: Vesterålen – Hinnøya Sør.

Start your multi-day walk from the car park by the **Ingelsfjordeidet** ❶. At first walk over boggy ground, at times with the help of wooden planks to overcome the worst areas. The clearly visible path brings you down to Storvatnet lake and continues further along the northern shoreline. After 1.2km the path turns northwards uphill and runs parallel to the Tverrelva river through the Forkledalen. Here, too, you will find wooden planks to help you make your way across the particularly boggy areas.

At a beautiful many-stepped waterfall the path leads you round to the left and leads up into a large boggy depression. You need to be careful when crossing the narrow planks that are present here – they are very slippery when it's wet or frosty.

Forkledalen is surrounded by the impressive massifs of Forkledalstindan, 902m, in the east and Sebortinden, 829m, in the southwest.

Right at the end of this expansive valley the path leads you up a few vertical metres above a small side valley; once you reach the top you meet the Tverrelva river again and enter Møysalen nasjonalpark. After crossing the little river ascend northwards into a high valley. The vegetation becomes more and more sparse. A few birch trees, Arctic willows and dwarf shrubs still hug the ground otherwise the terrain is increasingly stony.

You arrive at a mountain lake which you walk around on its right hand side. Your path is now less easy to detect on the stony and moss-covered

Waymarker at the edge of the path.

ground. Large areas are covered in snow here right into summer. You overcome a short incline up a scree gully onto the Forkledalsskaret col, 430m. The first foothill of Møysalen rises up ahead. The massif of the highest mountain of the Vesterålen and the island of Hinnøya towers majestically in front of you which will certainly tempt you to take the detour that is described as follows. You descend into the Møysaldalen with its turquoise-blue lake Midtre Møysalvatnet. After walking for a total of 6.5km you come to a junction of paths before the Midtre **Møysalvatnet** ❷. From here there are signposted routes to the Snytindhytta, as well as to Møysalen (4.5km) and to the Lonkanfjorden (5.5km).

Alternative: ascent of Møysalen, 1262m
You have the option at this point of climbing the highest mountain of Vesterålen and Hinnøya. The ascent leads you from the junction of paths in a northwesterly direction along a clearly visible path waymarked with cairns up to the col of Memuruskaret. From there continue your way as described in Walk 47. The grade (a 'black' walk) for the ascent is also mentioned in Walk 47 (the walking time only from the junction at Midtre Møysalvatnet and back again is a good 5 hrs, 1180 vertical metres).

From the **junction** ❷ set off in the direction of the Snytindhytta. Cairns and red waymarkers are sparingly placed and lead downhill to the lake of **Nedre Møysalvatnet** which you have to walk round on its eastern side up a steep and wet slope. Overcome a steep rocky section by the water by walking above it. An additional problem is caused by the fact that the path has now disappeared in places. At the end of the Nedre Møysalvatnet the terrain levels out and you turn your attention to the descent into the **Vestpolldalen** ❸.

Walk along the right hand side of a stream through a light wood with birch and ash trees and also dense ferns. The Vestpolldalen is a very wet valley with many side streams and bogs and drains the water from Møysalen via the Vestpollelva into the Vestpollen. In the absence of a bridge you have to ford the series of rivers. In early summer or after heavy rainfall the crossing of the whole valley is a very wet affair. To help you find your way across there are red waymarkers on the trees; a waterfall bubbling out of the opposite high valley serves as a basic point of orientation.

The path now becomes obvious again and leads you on the right of the waterfall across rock slabs up the slope. At the end of the rock slabs keep right again further on. The waterfall is now visible again and with another steep incline you come into the high valley lying ahead. This is a wide valley, open and also criss-crossed with many boggy sections. Looking back you can enjoy a fantastic view of the summit region of Møysalen which now lies behind you. From here onwards the path is once more well marked with cairns.

At the end of the valley climb up onto the next mountain ledge where Langvatnet lake is located, 424m, in a valley basin. At the latest from here you find yourself amidst the high alpine landscape of Hinnøya which will now accompany you for a long time. The drainage of Langvatnet lake takes place through a small gorge which you pass on your ascent. On account of a rock wall you cannot start to walk directly along the shoreline, but have to walk round it on the right hand side over the scree above. On your way look out for cairns and red T-waymarkers. At the end of the lake get your bearings by heading towards the lowest point, the **Sjettevasskaret** ❹.

Once you have reached the col you come to the border of the national park and on the right hand side you can see a huge cirque. Walk virtually

In the Vestpolldalen.

in a straight line down into the region of the **Småvatnene**, the 'small lakes' of Sjettevatnet, Femtevatnet and Fjerdevatnet. At the lakes walk in a westerly direction (on the left hand side) along the shoreline through the partly scree-covered and meadow area. The lakes are flanked in the east by the elongated massif of Snøtindan (also called Snytindan) which consists of several peaks. Nordtinden, 883m, rises in the west. At the end of the third lake, Fjerdevatnet, cross over a river by means of a bridge. After that it's a tedious 1.5km long walk across muddy and also rocky terrain with patches of dwarf birch trees. The large impressive lake of Øvre Blokkvatnet (also called Trivatnet) lies on your left.

After having completed about 17km, you come to the **Snytindhytta** ❺ of the Vesterålen Turlag (VT). The unstaffed mountain hut consists of two buildings with a total of 22 sleeping places, a roomy kitchen/living space in the large main building and a sauna. It stands amidst a wonderful location surrounded by some small and some larger lakes and high mountain peaks. To the south in the distance you can see Møysalen whose summit is about a 16km long walk from from this point.

In the Forkledalen.

Alternatives:

There are various options for extending this walk from the mountain hut which go in three directions: either, set off to the west to the **Djupfjorden**. The walk along this path is described in reverse direction in Walk 49. It is a very well marked and beautiful stage of 11km in length.
Or a second possibility is the similarly well-marked 9km walk across the Løbergdalsskaret and then eastwards through the **Løbergsdalen** to the Rv 85 on the Løbergsbukta (Gullesfjorden). This path is very wet after heavy rainfall and in early summer.

At the mountain hut choose the well-trodden path marked with red Ts and cairns to the Sigerfjorden and so you start off by climbing the first kilometre across rocky terrain up to the **Løbergdalsskaret col**. Turn to the left on the col (junction of paths with signposts) northwards. The path into the Løbergsdalen continues straight ahead (see Alternative). Ascend the southern flank of Breidtindaksla. Once you arrive at the top you are standing in front of a valley basin where, way down below, you can see Breidtindvatnet lake.
It's a leisurely ascent up the slope lying on your right and you come to another col over which you reach the upper end of Vangpolldalen. From here you can enjoy distant views across the large lake of Øvre Vangpollvatnet.

After crossing another hillside the 735m high Djupfjordtindan appears opposite you standing at the eastern end of the lake. A short incline brings you onto the ridge lying ahead. Once on the ridge you have now reached the highest point, at an altitude of 730m, of your multi-day trip – assuming that you haven't walked to the top of Møysalen. Ascend the ridge onto **Vangpollskaret col** ❻.

Turn northeastwards here and descend a broad ridge leisurely down to the cirque lake of Rundvatnet. Opposite lies the broad and distinctive Tverrelvtindan. With its height of 1118m it towers over the Tverrelvdalen. From the cirque lake it goes down another high step to Storvatnet lake (also called Tverelvvatnan). The vegetation now increases, the first low willows and birch trees line the path, and a more dense covering of grass. The mountain chain belonging to Stortinden (Walk 50) accompanies you on the left hand side. The path runs comfortably along the western shoreline of the Storvatnet. At the place where the lake drains into the Tverrelvdalen you cross over a small bridge. At the end of the lake ascend once more onto a small col to then descend to another small lake.

The going gets more tedious now since the path is becoming increasingly stony and wet. Walk past the lake on the left and over the Sørheia hill, 310m. From here it is relatively easy on the knees as you walk across the ground of soft peat through the heath-covered landscape and a light birchwood. The walk ends at the **car park** ❼ on the Fv 822.

Lunch break at the side of the path.

49 Snytindhytta, 390m

↗ 800m | ↘ 800m | 20.8km
7.30 hrs

Delightful walk in the alpine setting of Hinnøya

There is an abundance of walks on the island of Hinnøya with alpine character. The Snytindhytta is reached after an uphill trek of 11km, far away from civilisation. This mountain hut can be chosen for an overnight stop on a multi-day walk or as a base for further exploration of the local surroundings. Apart from the route we describe here there are three other approaches to the mountain hut. The Snytindhytta is also a popular destination for ski tours.

Starting point: Djupfjord, gravel path with parking places on the Fv 822, 30m. On the Fv 822 coming from Sigerfjord a gravel path turns off left 800m after the Djupfjord bridge (over the Djupfjorden).
Grade: well-marked footpath (red waymarkers, cairns), with large muddy sections and partly rocky terrain. Waterproof shoes are a must.
Infrastructure: unstaffed Snytindhytta of the Vesterålen Turlag (information at vesteralen.dnt.no).
Alternatives: there are three further approaches to the Snytindhytta: from the Ingelsfjordeidet on the E 10 (about 17km); from the Løbergsbukta (on the Rv 85) through the Løbergsdalen (9km) and also east of the Sigerfjord (Rv 85) past Stortinden and Tverrelvtindan (10.5km). Møysalen lies about 16km away from the Snytindhytta (also see Walk 48).
Map: Vesterålen – Hinnøya Sør.

Reward at the end of your walk – polar lights over the Snytindhytta.

Start your walk from the car park at **Djupfjord** ❶ with a 4km long section along the gravel road above the Djupfjorden. After the first two kilometres there's a turn-off (signpost) and you follow the forest road to the right. Hallskogvatnet lake now lies on the right hand side way down below, hidden behind a dense group of trees.

In order to find the next junction of the footpath you now need a certain amount of concentration. If you arrive at the end of the gravel road at the wall of the dammed lake you have gone about 150m too far.

So you need to pay special attention here – when the forest road ascends slightly to the left round a bend you will see a track on the left hand side which leads to a gate in the rock. About 50m further on an inconspicuous path on the right turns off into the area of meadows and boggy areas. This is the path you need to take.

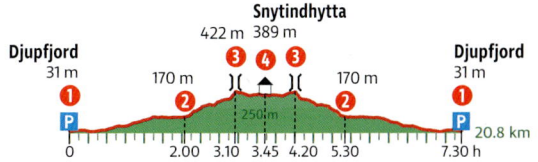

Walk around a range of hills and reach the westernmost bay of **Storvatnet**. Walk here along a narrow and stony path across the hillside beside the southern shoreline. The vegetation is very dense and luxuriant and consequently very wet. Head towards a peninsula where you'll find a large **boulder** ❷ by the lakeside – an ideal spot to stop for a rest.

The path continues in a southeasterly direction in a wet valley with extensive boggy areas (no wooden planks for bridges) up several high ledges as far as Beibarnsvatnan lake. Walk across the concrete dam at the overflow of the lake and continue on its eastern side. Up another two levels along beside a stream, a lake, across marshes and berries you come to a small **col** ❸. The two Isvatnet lakes lie ahead surrounded by mountains like in an amphitheatre. You slowly descend the rocky terrain bordered by low shrubs and boggy ground. A last short incline brings you up to the beautifully located **Snytindhytta** ❹.

The mountain hut is located amidst an alpine and rocky landscape scattered with blueberry bushes, surrounded by lakes and up to 900m high mountain peaks. In the southwest you can make out the prominent summit of the 1262m high Møysalen. If you choose to stay overnight, two cosy huts and a fantastic night sky await you. Otherwise you return the same way to Djupfjord ❶.

Amidst the mountains and yet so close to the water.

↗ 1010m | ↘ 1010m | 5.1km
4.30 hrs

Stortinden, 1021m 50

A summit of superlatives

The 1021m high Stortinden is climbed in a fabulous ascent of only 2.35km. Nowhere else on Vesterålen and the Lofoten do you come onto a summit of this altitude in such a short distance. Consequently the ascent is very steep and not everyone's cup of tea. The panorama from the summit is spectacular and particularly breathtaking is the view into the high alpine landscape of Hinnøya.

Starting point: parking bay on the Vangpollen, 10m. From the Rv 85 shortly before or just after – depending on which way you are coming – the Sigerfjord tunnel turn off onto the Fv 822 in the direction of Kaljorda. After 3.7km (about 200m before the hydroelectric plant) there are small parking bays on the right and the left.
Grade: steep, strenuous walk in mostly stony and/or scree-covered terrain. Some cairns in places.
Infrastructure: campsite, accommodation, restaurants, supermarkets and petrol stations in Sortland. Petrol station as well as a supermarket in Kjerringnes and Strand.
Tip: if you would like a closer look at the high alpine areas of Hinnøya, you should consider following the walk to the Snytindhytta (Walk 49).
Map: Vesterålen – Hinnøya Sør.

On top at last.

You can make out your destination already from the car park at **Vangpollen** ❶. Looking in a southeasterly direction you can see, on the right, the dominating Vangpollheia, 692m, and on the left of it a high valley that doesn't have a name and the adjoining massif of Stortinden. The clearly visible and well-trodden path runs for the first 350m through a wooded boggy area.

After that it's a steep uphill climb. A tedious ascent brings you up a path covered in tree roots and stones. When you stop to catch your breath, which you will need to do regularly, look back for an ever widening view. Way below you can see the Vangpollen (on the left) and the Austpollen (on the right) which are the two ends of the Sigerfjorden, as well as the Vangpollneset peninsula. Also visible in the distance is the large asphalt works

The summit is within reach.

in Husvik. From a height of 400m the vegetation becomes increasingly thinner. You are now walking on the left flank of the high valley which you could already see from the car park, and you come onto a rocky **hill** ❷. Way over in the west you can see the huge massif of the Djupfjordtindan, 891m, as well as the arc of the three peaks of Viktinden, Middagsbogtinden and Brokløystinden while in the northwest, the Sigerfjorden is visible and also the village of Sigerfjord and the Sortlandsundet. Opposite and to the north of you, stands the Gårdsdalstinden, 786m, the mountain through which the Sigerfjord tunnel runs. The municipality of Sigerfjord (about 700 inhabitants) lived and still does make its living from the fishing industry. At the turn of the 19th, the shipping company of Hindø Dampskibsselskap A/S located here and in so doing gave the town a new lease of life. Today Sigerfjord Fiske A/S is a well-known producer of Arctic char (ishavsrøye). Sigerfjord gained unhappy notoriety on 7th March, 1956. On that day, the Vesterålen and Lofoten were hit by several avalanches in which a total of 20 people died. In Sigerfjord 9 children and 4 adults were killed in their homes. The terrible memory of this accident is still very much alive today among the survivors.

If you look into the direction of your ascent, you can see the flank leading up to the Stortinden. Your path, which now runs mostly through scree,

initially runs along below the ridge and bypasses steep rocky terrain on the right. Then it continues up a steep incline towards the upper edge of the ridge. Relatively close to this edge ascend to the **summit ❸**, the last metres through rubble. Once at the top, you can enjoy an impressive 360 degree panorama overlooking Hinnøya, Norway's largest island, with its various mountains and fjords, and also the Langøya mountain range to the west. The most impressive, however, is the high alpine landscape extending southwards around Møysalen, 1262m (Walks 47–49).

Return the same path to the **Vangpollen ❶**.

Summit view from Stortinden.

↗ 840m | ↘ 840m | 11.1km
4.30 hrs

51 Skata, 736m

Between Eidsfjorden and Sortlandssundet

Skata is a majestic summit in the middle of the mountain range located in the main part of Langøya island. It rises up in the shape of a pyramid from a chain of mountains. This strenuous and long path is compensated by fantastic views across beautiful fjord scenery and the alpine mountains of Vesterålen.

Starting point: car park at the end of a roadway in Rise, 25m. On the Fv 82 (12.6km south of Sortlandsbrua, 10.7km north of Hadselbrua) turn off onto a roadway that is signposted to 'Turløyper', drive past a house on the right and then continue for another 450m into the valley where you keep left and park at the gate.
Grade: demanding walk on unmarked paths, with a few cairns in places; some boy scout skills are definitely needed with route finding in some of the sections; a lack of vertigo and surefootedness are absolutely necssary on the ridge.
Infrastructure: accommodation, campsite, supermarkets and petrol stations in Stokmarknes and Sortland.
Tip: the roadway from the car park leads to Risvatnet which is a recreational area with opportunities for fishing, fire pits and toilets.
Map: Vesterålen – Hinnøya Sør.

On Skata.

Start from the car park in **Rise** ❶ and immediately walk through the gate and turn left along beside electricity power lines. There are some old wooden signposts indicating the way at first and then you come through another gate. The roadway gradually narrows and becomes more and more stony underfoot. After a gentle incline you meet another **roadway** ❷. Follow this roadway to the right into a valley. On the left hand side below lies a large boggy area. At the **end of the roadway** ❸ continue straight ahead towards the hillside. Since the whole area is a pasture for sheep in the summer there are numerous tracks criss-crossing the land. Some plastic bands have been fastened to trees and these guide you up the steep slope. It's not really a path in the real sense of the word, but the waymarker bands help you find your way up the grassy hillside where there are no paths.

At the end of the slope you come onto a small **hill** ❹. Looking back you have a beautiful view of Hinnøya lying opposite and the northern foothills of Austvågøya. A narrow, but obvious path begins here once more which leads up a gentle slope and on its way swings round to the left. With another left hand bend you reach the edge of the next plateau. There's the occasional cairn to help guide you along. Now, on the left hand side, walk round a large boggy area.

In search of the sun.

You can see the ridge leading up to Skata ahead. A large cirque opens up below where the mountain lakes of Gluntvatnet and Litlevatnet are located. Since the path loses itself again you have to find your way across the boggy areas and in so doing head towards the hill **P. 445** ❺ where you can see a cairn. This is the point you are aiming for.

From the hill there's an intermediary descent onto a col. After that you reach the first ridge where the path continues and is now exposed. After another short descent you cross through a notch from which you look down northwards into the valley of the little Lahaugelva river and to the south towards the Storvatnet, Litlevatnet and Gluntvatnet lakes. Then follows an area of meadowland and from here it's still a good 130 vertical metres until you reach the top of **Skata** ❻ from which a fantastic panorama opens out across the Vesterålen revealing all its alpine peaks. The highest mountain of the archipelago, Møysalen, towers up in the southeast with an impressive altitude of 1262m.

Return on the same path. On your descent from the hill **P. 445** ❺ you can easily be misled into following the sheep tracks which are considerably more well-trodden on the eastern side and walking round the boggy area on the left. If you do this, however, you can rejoin the correct path later on, but then you have to walk across rough ground without any paths.

↗ 450m | ↘ 450m | 8.2km
2.30 hrs

Veten, 467m | 52

A family walk par excellence

A not very steep incline leads through a secluded little wood along an historical path. On the way there's a cabin where you can stop for a while and from here the summit is easy to reach.

Starting point: Steine, walkers' car park, 14m, 700m east of the Fv 820. Turn off in the centre of the village.
Grade: easy, waymarked footpath with moderate inclines.
Infrastructure: info at boe.kommune.no. Supermarkets in Straume and Vinje. Petrol station in Straume.
Alternative: continue from the summit of Veten to Lynghaugtinden, 504m, and descend to Føre (2.15 hrs, 7.5km, 210m in ascent, 660m in descent, a 'red' walk): from Veten a tiny path (cairns) runs in a northerly direction across a broad high plateau to Lynghaugtinden. Your descent continues from Lynghaugtinden in a southwesterly direction following the sign for Nøkbua through a dense conifer wood and along a forest track as far as the Fv 820 in Føre. On the opposite side of the road you can walk further on to the burial site in Føre. It's 8km back along the road to your starting point so you would need a bike or a second car from here.
Tips: the Mannen fra havet, which is part of the Skulpturlandskap Nordland art project, stands in Vinje. The small Bø Museum is also closeby.
The Svinøya islands are located off the coast at Vinje where you will find a collection of graves, 130 in total, dating back as far as the Iron Age (reachable at low tide if you want to keep your feet dry).
In Føre there's an interesting burial site dating back to the 5th century.
The delightful and distinctive islands of Gaukværøya and Litløya with Litløy fyr (the lighthouse offers exclusive overnight stops) are only reachable by boat.
Map: Vesterålen – Hinnøya Sør.

The Losjehytta of the local walking association – a lovely spot for a rest.

Occasionally you'll pass a welcome wind shelter – here on the top of Veten.

From the walkers' car park in **Steine** ❶ follow the sign for Veten/Losjehytta along a gravel path that becomes an old roadway after a sheep fence. After 10 minutes you are standing on a low col. There's an engraving here on a stone, as well as an information board, relating to the old church path you find yourself walking along here that was constructed in 1840 from Vinje to the church in Bø. The old path runs down to the sea across a muddy depression to the church (from 1824).

Follow the red waymarkers and continue to ascend the broad path below the mountain hillside of Steinmelen to the **Losjehytta** ❷, the cabin belonging to the local walking association. The cosy little cabin stands at the

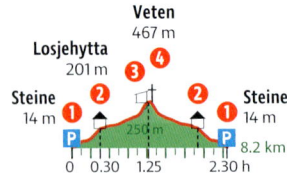
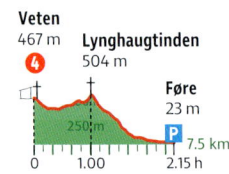

edge of a grove of trees and is an inviting place to stop for a rest (there's a spring where you can collect water a few metres to the north beside the path). A short detour brings you along a narrow path southwestwards onto the summit of **Steinmelen**, 265m, from where there's a wonderful panorama of the Lofoten opposite.

Now walk across an extensive area of boogy ground. On the way you pass some signposts with alternative approaches and then ascend a broad mountain ridge towards the summit. A short steep climb at the end and you have reached the shelter **Vetenhytta** ❸ and just 80 metres further on to the northeast, the summit of **Veten** ❹. From here you can savour the view across the municipality of Bø and its offshore islands towards the Lofoten.

Walk back down the same way to **Steine** ❶.

↗ 620m | ↘ 620m | 7.9km
3.00 hrs

53 Breitinden, 598m

Walk beside the Eidsfjorden

The Breitinden stretches up from the Eidsfjorden above the many skerries of Guvåg, ascending between the Hellfjorden and the Jarnfjorden. According to legend a troll once dug out the Eidsfjorden since, in his opinion, the Vesterålen consisted of too many mountains. He was digging for so long that his spade (ræka) broke. In his rage he threw it away from him and the invincible looking wall of Reka/Goivo rises today where the spade landed, and the handle of the spade became the island of Rekøya.

But humans have always lived by water which is rich in fish. In the second half of the 19th century the Eidsfjorden became the centre of a 'Gold Rush' of the Vesterålen: what the cod was to the Lofotingers, herring was to the Eidsfjorders – 400,000 barrels of salted herring in one season and an Eidsfjorden dripping with herring fat.

Starting point: Guvåg, on the Fv 7654, 18m. Parking places around the harbour. From here walk 500m back along the road and the footpath starts on the right before a house after the big left hand bend and before the next small right hand bend.
Grade: easily visible path, in some places with old T-waymarkers and cairns. Some shortish sections can be boggy or stony.
Infrastructure: information at boe.kommune.no. Supermarket and petrol station in Straume. The locked, unstaffed Guvåghytta of the Vesterålen Turlag is located by the coast (information at vesteralen.dnt.no).
Map: Vesterålen – Hinnøya Sør.

Start your walk from the middle of **Guvåg** ❶ and take the well-trodden path past a house across an area of meadow. You are soon walking slowly, but continuously uphill. Shortly after the meadows walk through a light wood and an area of bushes. The higher you come, the more you imagine what kind of view awaits you from the top. From about 200m upwards

Breitinden is a popular walkers' destination on the Vesterålen.

leave the wooded area behind and walk through an extensive heath-covered landscape. On your leisurely ascent you cross over **Vindhammaren** ❷ and continue over a gently undulating plateau with shrubby heath and boggy patches. Your path now leads you after the boggy areas in a westerly direction up the hillside below the scree slopes until, at a height of 370m, it swerves to the east round a hairpin bend.

A good 150m further on turn to the north (cairns) and ascend the next 150m more or less in a straight line directly to the top. On the last few vertical metres cross over to the edge of Breitinden ridge to then immediately climb up along it again heading northwest to the pre-summit. Now it's only another few paces to reach the summit plateau of **Breitinden** ❸. From here you can see the continuation of the mountain chain which no longer runs broadly, but precipitously from now on to the north, while below there's a view across the Eidsfjorden to the shoreline on the opposite side which also belongs to the island of Langøya. **Return** the same path to **Guvåg** ❶.

↗ 180m | ↘ 180m | 5.0km
1.30 hrs

54 Vikan

Coastal walk on Norway's oldest rock

This easy hike takes you over greyish green gneis which is 2.7 billion years old and therefore Norway's oldest visible rock strata. A beautiful coastal path brings you to two navigational lights and (if you decide to extend the walk) to one of the most delightful sandy beaches on Vesterålen.

Starting point: Handkleppan, 6m, car park. At the roundabout in Straume leave the Fv 820 in the direction of Straumsjøen, keep right here and you will find parking places at the end of a settlement of rorbuer.
Grade: easy walk for the whole family, with T-waymarkers, stony ground between the two navigational lights and protective handrails in places.
Infrastructure: info at boe.kommune.no. Supermarket and petrol station in Straume.
Alternative: continue the walk from ❸, see p. 208 for the description.
Tips: if you continue along the Fv 820 in the direction of Vinje you will come to Føre. The burial site there dating back to the 5th century is well worth a visit. The Mannen fra havet which is part of the art project of the Skulpturlandskap Nordland is located in Vinje and the small Bø Museum is just nearby.
The offshore islands of Svinøya lie in front of Vinje – there are 130 graves from the Iron Age which can be reached at low tide without getting your feet wet.
Map: Vesterålen – Hinnøya Sør.

The walk leads through a beautiful coastal landscape with remains of old settlements.

Start your walk from the car park in **Handkleppan** ❶ and pass a white house brought here in the 60s from Åsand. The roadway dating back to the 30s leads to the old settlement of **Vikan** whose remaining buildings are only used these days as summerhouses. The following footpath across the area of meadows brings you to **Sørleia** ❷ navigational light. 600 metres further north you can see Flaskforet, the next light. At first the path runs through the stony coastal region. Then on the following steeply sloping meadow there are some protective handrails. If you scramble over the rocky beach lower down within the tide line, you will discover glacial potholes, also known as giant's kettles (jettegryter). Eventually you arrive on a broad **rocky plateau** ❸ where the first part of the coastal walk comes to

an end. The **Flaskforet** navigational light stands just offshore on a small promontory where a bit of scrambling is needed in order to reach it.
Return the way you came. The walk can be extended by following the alternative route described below.

Alternative: continuation of the coastal walk from ❸ via Digerneset, Kjerringstranda (gapahuk), Åsand and Spjelkvågen to the Fv 820 (3.00 hrs, 7.6km, 300 vertical metres, a 'red' walk; few waymarkers)
The end point of this walk is close to the Fv 820 – in order to return to the **car park** ❶ it's a good idea to have left a bike here.
The path is, to start with, clearly visible as it ascends the hillside covered in bushes. Between **Digerneset** and **Kjerringstranda** a wide valley opens up on the right hands side. According to the map there ought to be a path across the Spikarheia from here to Handkleppan, but we have never found it. The rest of the path to Åsand, where 1500 years ago there was already a settlement with a fantastic sandy beach, is extremely rough and demands absolute surefootedness and route finding skills on the steep, stony and also grass and bush covered, hillside. The settlement of **Åsand** was abandoned in the 60s and there are a few foundation walls still to be found here. The wonderful sandy beach is an attractive bathing spot and a popular stopping off point for the Arctic Sea Kayak Race which takes place every year.
A path that is not always obvious runs over varying terrain – meadows, scree, fen – into **Spjelkvågen bay**. The last kilometre is along a gravel roadway that takes you to a car park just before the Fv 820.

On Åsand beach.

If you look carefully you might even discover jettegryter.

↗ 140m | ↘ 140m | 1.8km
0.45 hrs

55 Bufjellet, 210m

Unimposing rock at the 'end of the world'

Bufjellet is an inconspicuous rock with a completely special atmosphere. It nestles between the Norwegian Sea and a landscape of moraine and together with its offshore islands is home to thousands of sea birds during breeding time. It is a bare landscape through which you climb to the top. Walking in between rock formations and stones you have the feeling of being in a playground for trolls.
There's a wonderful view of the midnight sun from here in summer and you can listen to the birds' making their racket while in the colder seasons, there's only the sound of the breaking waves as you gaze at the night sky and, with a bit of luck, the polar lights too.

Starting point: Sandvikhalsen, 75 m, parking bay on the col between Sandvika and Nykvåg on the Fv 7656.
Grade: the path is waymarked in places with cairns; easy incline all the way up.
Infrastructure: info at boe.kommune.no. Supermarket and petrol station in Straume. Café in Hovden in summer.
Tip: the fishing villages of Nykvåg and Hovden brave defy the rough Norwegian Sea. Between the two places there's a landscape of terminal moraines: the stony beach is some of the oldest sedimentation in Norway. In Hovden you've reached the 'end of the world' – just watch, listen and enjoy…
Map: Vesterålen – Hinnøya Sør.

From **Sandvikhalsen col** ❶ start your walk up to Bufjellet in a northwesterly direction.
Walk up the path across the hillside which is covered in scree and starts off ascending gently. At times there are several paths running parallel to one another and just the occasional

Glacial coastal landscape between Nykvåg and Hovden, with Bufjellet in the background.

Magical moments – polar lights above the bird rocks.

cairn. However, the direction is always obvious – just keep walking uphill so that, after 20 minutes, you are already standing on the highest elevation (210m) of the elongated **Bufjellet** ❷. From the western edge you have a good view of Sandvikbukta bay and the offshore bird islands of Engenyken, Måsnyken and Spjøten. The 3556 hectares of the large Nykvåg/Nykan nature reserve also begin here which is a breeding territory for common guillemots, black-legged kittiwakes, razorbills and Atlantic puffins. Before making your return you might want to continue for a while across the extensive Bufjellet which stretches further to the north and walk as far as the view down to Nykvåg bay and the fishing villages of Nykvåg and Vågen. There's no longer a definite path now. Just find your way between the sheep and the rocky edge of the hill across the grass-covered, at times stony heia.
Return the same path.

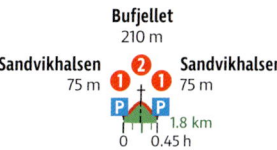

↗ 560m | ↘ 560m | 6.3km

56 Trollan, 543m

2.50 hrs

High up above one of the most beautiful places on Vesterålen

A gnome once sneaked onto the bog to steal the cloudberries from the trolls. There was a tussle which lasted until the early hours of the morning. As he escaped to the sea the gnome was petrified by the rising sun. He can now be seen as the Tussen mountain at an altitude of 198m on the way to Hovden. The trolls were also petrified, however, and today they stand towering above the Tussen. The fishing villages of Nykvåg and Hovden defy the rough Norwegian Sea. You pass through a landscape of terminal moraines between these two places where the stony beach is some of the oldest rock strata in Norway. In Hovden you have reached the 'end of the world' where you can only watch, listen and enjoy.

On the way to the summit of Trollan.

Starting point: car park at Ravatnet lake, 14m. About 1.5km east of Nykvåg on the Fv 7656 towards Hovden, a roadway branches off to the right. Alternatively, there is another possibility to park your car 100m before.
Grade: the path is clearly visible, no waymarkers, the start of the path and the path to the summit can be a bit difficult to find.
Infrastructure: info at boe.kommune.no. Supermarket and petrol station in Straume. Café in Hovden in summer.
Remarks: if you use the walks suggestion marked on the hiking map across Røsshagheia and Selvågtinden, 568m, you will be walking predominantly on sheep paths or even over rough ground across patches of meadow covered in dwarf shrubs. The descent runs for the most part through boggy areas with no path at all.
Map: Vesterålen – Hinnøya Sør.

Start your walk from the point where the **roadway** ❶ turns off from the Fv 7656, pass through a meadow gate and cross under a power line. The hillside of Siktartinden dominates your view on the left hand side. The lakes of Ravatnet and Toftvatnet, the two lowest of a chain of glacial lakes, lie on your right hand side. After about 500m you come to a giant-sized **boulder** ❷ standing on the left of the path. A faintly visible path leads past the left hand side of the rock and after another 5m bends to the right (fairly visible). On your left you will now come to a hill, 130m in height, which is covered in large scree slopes. The path leads you eastwards and along below a scree slope. After that continue steeply up at times round

If you reach the small harbour in Hovden your thoughts drift across the Norwegian Sea towards Greenland.

zigzag bends that lead over a mountain ridge to a **rocky spur** ❸. Looking back you have a beautiful view downhill of the moraine landscape below. In the Nykdalen the glacial lakes (paternoster lakes) lie gleaming in a row just like a string of pearls.

The path now continues more gently along a ridge-like edge and the ground falls away to become a broad ridge. The rock formations of Siktartinden, 444m, are on your left. A good 300m afterwards keep along the northern edge where the path leads between a few boulders to the blocky summit of **Trollan** ❹. There are sheep tracks in the summit area so that route finding can prove to be a bit tricky. When the path fails, just find your way across the stretches of heathland covered in dense bushes of cloudberries towards the highest point. **Return** the same way to the **starting point** ❶.

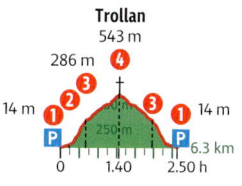

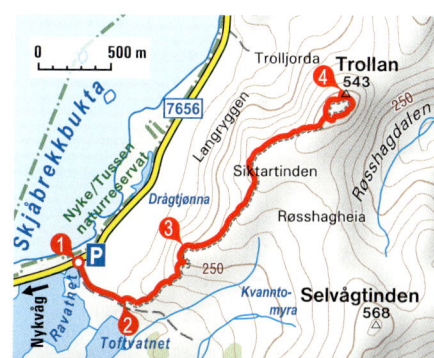

↗ 600m | ↘ 600m | 7.3km
3.15 hrs

57 Nonskollen, 611m

🚌

A wonderful mountain bathed in the light of the midnight sun

An easy and quick walk with views over a landscape of salt marshes and peatlands can be made in the north of Nonskollen as well as to the mountain regions of Langøya and Hinnøya that lies in the far distance. The Grunnfjorden nature reserve protects a wetland area of 17,724 hectares according to the Ramsar convention which is an internationally important agreement on wetlands, in particular as a habitat for water and wading birds. Large parts of the peatlands of Storemyra, the Grunnfjorden and also parts of the island of Gisløya and its adjoining wetlands offer a protected habitat all year round for peat bogs, salt marshes, a lagoon of brackish water, beach biotopes and various water birds during their breeding and migratory periods. It is possible to watch greater scaups, ruffs, knots, whooper swans, dunlins, ruddy turnstones and golden plovers.

Starting point: Alsvåg, parking in front of the school, 10m. On the Fv 7674 coming from Myre, it is left at the village entrance.
Grade: clear and visible path with moderate inclines.
Infrastructure: accommodation and restaurants in Myre, Nyksund, Stø and Toften (visitvesteralen.com). Supermarket in Alsvåg and Myre. Petrol station in Myre.
Tip: the Øksnes Museum in Alsvåg is an interesting place to visit and is located in the old warehouse of the Ålsvåg farm. You can go on bird and seal safaris from Stø and Nyksund as well as boat trips for whale watching (seasafarioksnes.no, arcticwhaletours.no).
On the island of Meløya (signposted), you can go on walks along the beach and swim in the Norwegian Sea (parking at the cemetery).
Map: Vesterålen – Hinnøya Sør.

From the parking area at the school in **Alsvåg** ❶ walk along the road for just under 180m until you are nearly at the first house. A power line turns off to the right and a roadway leads

Midnight glow on Nonskollen.

to the Alsvåg cross country ski track which brings you across the Alsvåg fen. After about 600m you come to a pasture fence and a gravel path that continues westwards. Follow this path for a few metres and then turn left onto a footpath to the **ski lift** ❷. Ascend the mountain hillside below the ski lift. At the end of the line of light towers keep to the left and continue your walk leisurely through a thin forest of birch trees. The path now leads you up the broad mountain ridge lying ahead to the summit of **Nonskollen** ❸. From here you can look northwards across the Alsvågvatnet lake to the prominent cone-shaped summit of Sørvågmelen, 313m, the boggy areas of Stormyra and the most northerly foothills of Langøya as well as the Norwegian Sea. To the east you can also see the southern part of Andøya island and a part of Hinnøya too while your view to the south and west stretches into infinity along the mountain formations of Langøya and Hinnøya.
Return the same path to **Alsvåg** ❶.

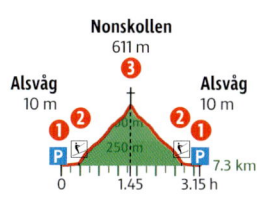

TOP 58 — ↗ 1000m | ↘ 1000m | 15.3km
Dronningruta – the queen's route
5.30 hrs

Queen Sonja's favourite walk

The Dronningruta owes its name to Norway's Queen Sonja who has been hiking in the Vesterålen for many years. On this 15 kilometre walk which was voted Norway's most beautiful hike in 2012 you can experience everything that Vesterålen has to offer: a delightful coastline on the Norwegian Sea, sandy beaches, steep mountains, fantastic panoramic views and two charmingly quaint fishing villages. It is hard to believe, but with 250 inhabitants, Nyksund was once one of the most important fishing villages in the Vesterålen. In the course of the motorisation of the fishing industry, however, the place lost importance and in 1970 fell into a deep sleep. After various attempts at reviving the village, Nyksund is now re-emerging and has been turned into a jewel of the Vesterålen, especially with the help of German nationals who have come to live here over the past few years.

Starting point: Skåltofta, walkers' car park, 26m, 1km before you reach Nyksund. Alternative parking and access directly from Nyksund.

The interior of the church in Langenes.

Grade: well marked footpath; large patches of boggy land along the coastline; on the high paths there are sections protected with ropes and you might also need to use your hands in places; some stony areas and heathland. The whole circular walk constitutes a demanding full day's walk.

Infrastructure: a variety of restaurants and accommodation in Nyksund (nyksund.no). In Stø there's a caravan camping site and a few rorbuer as well as a café. Supermarket and petrol station in Myre.

Alternatives: there is an option to walk just part of this route, e.g. the stretch from Nyksund along the coastal path as far as Stø (2 hrs, 5.5km, 240 vertical metres). However you will need to organise a lift (or leave a second car at the end point, or a bike) for the return along the 23km long road to your starting point in Nyksund. There is also a possibility of pre-booking a boat to transfer you back to Nyksund (seasafarioksnes.no).

Tips: from Stø and Nyksund, you can go on a bird and seal safari or a whale

watching trip (seasafarioksnes.no, arctic-whaletours.no).
This walk as well as the villages of Nyksund and Stø are ideal places from which to watch the course of the midnight sun.

In the neighbouring village of Langenes there's an interesting church that's worth a visit which was built at the beginning of the 16th century and is therefore the oldest church on the Vesterålen.
Map: Vesterålen – Hinnøya Sør.

From the walkers' car park in **Skåltofta** ❶ you start immediately by walking up onto the small hill lying ahead. At the top you are standing before a chain of lakes that form the reservoir for Nyksund's drinking water. The well marked path leads you onto the broad ridge between the mountains of Nyken and Mælen. From here continue onto the southern flank of Mælen, ascending straight on higher and higher until you reach the ridge ahead. From here continue gently down the slope onto **Nyksundskaret col** ❷.

The following path runs in a southeasterly direction along the ridge where you have to use your hands in a few places. The path changes over onto the northern side of the ridge where some sections are protected with a rope. Shortly afterwards you are standing on the large high plateau of Sløymarkheia from where you can enjoy an impressive panorama: in the southwest across the lakes of Nyksundvatnan and further on over the Prestfjorden as far as the coast of Skogsøya island. In the east below you is the valley basin of the Langvaddal while opposite you can see the line of mountains where your route continues to Stø.

It's a leisurely walk across the high plateau in the direction of **Finngamheia** ❸. From the top descend gently down the slope to the **col** ❹ below Sørkulen, 518m. Those who fancy a challenge can bag the summit of Sørkulen (no paths in places, across scree and through boulders).

Cross the northwestern flank of Sørkulen on the level with a view of the Langvaddalsvatnan lakes below. With a bit of gentle up and down continue along the mountain chain and over **Kjølen** ❺ which is the highest point of your walk. From here the path continues northeastwards with breathtaking views on the way down to the white sandy beach of Skipssanden. Finally you have reached the mountain of Kvalaksla where the radar station dominates the landscape. Then follows a steep descent bringing you down to **Stø** ❻.

Once you have reached the tarmac road turn left and you will see the signposted path back to Nyksund shortly before the Stø Bobilcamp. The waymarked path brings you across wet areas of meadowland and a few rocky ledges to Skipssanden beach which is a popular place for swimming in the summer and was already visible from above. After walking over a small hill continue across extensive marshy and boggy areas close to and parallel to the coastline to the stony beach. Along the way you come past the shelter (gapahuk) at Enge. The valley of Langvaddal opens up on your left hand side and the path runs along a ridge between a fresh water lake and the Norwegian Sea to a small settlement of huts.

After the huts you now start up the stony incline through a small forest of birch trees onto **Nyksundskaret col** ❷ where you stood at the beginning of the walk. From here return to the walkers' car park **Skåltofta** ❶. A visit to the restaurant or the café in Nyksund will be a great finish to the walk.

View from Finngamheia towards Gisløya and the southern tip of Andøya.

↗ 510m | ↘ 510m | 8.0km
2.45 hrs

59 Coastal paths between Stave and Bleik

An attractive network of paths at the northern tip of Andøya

Paths to remote bays and an extensive plateau high above the sandy beaches invite you to take shortish or longish walks. Just off the coast of this popular walking area lies the island of Bleiksøya, a breeding area for thousands of Atlantic puffins and other bird species. Even sea eagles like it here too. Just nearby you will find the 2.5km long sandy beach of Bleik to which it is thought that the town owes its name: 'Bleikr' means 'white' and 'light-coloured' in Old Norse. It is one of the longest and most beautiful sandy beaches in Norway. The 2.5km wide Bleik moraine lies to the southwest of the village and is 20,000 years old and Norway's oldest terminal moraine. Archaeological finds have shown that, on the one hand, this area was not covered in ice in the last Ice Age and, on the other hand, was already inhabited several thousand years ago. On the walk to Måtinden you will discover pit traps from the Stone Age. Archaeological discoveries in Stave are evidence of cereal being cultivated in the Middle Ages and in Høyvika you will come across the remains of settlements of more recent origin. The little hamlet of Bleik also has a special feature. Since people only had a limited settlement area and even after the drainage of the boggy areas they did not relocate their closely spaced houses, but instead continued to construct new buildings in the centre of the village, Bleik consists of a compact and narrow development. This makes it one of the few 'real' villages in Norway.

There are still thousands of puffins on Bleiksøya.

At the steep precipitous edge of Måtinden.

Starting point: Baugtua, 75m. Baugtua walkers' car park is located on the Fv 7702 between Bleik and Stave on a flat col in the Stavedalen.
Alternative 1 and 2: Laupsvika, 10m. Laupsvika bay is about 1.5km southwest of the harbour in Bleik and can be reached from Bleik along a roadway at the end of which you will find places to park.
Alternative 3: Skjåberget, 7m. North of Stave take the turning to Skjåberget and follow the gravel road right to the end.
The walks are described as there and back walks, summit crossings and linear walks. It is also possible to link them together to make a circular walk but that depends on your fitness and the extra time it will take. Sometimes you will need to organise a transfer (bike, second car).
Grade: easy walk on waymarked paths with moderate inclines. In low-lying cloud or fog you need to take special care as you can easily lose your way on the high plateau. The alternative routes are more demanding walks (see the description details). The alternative walks are not to be recommended in wet weather as the terrain becomes slippery and tricky to walk on.
Infrastructure: camping, accommodation, restaurants in Andenes, Bleik and Stave. Supermarkets in Bleik and Andenes. Petrol station in Andenes.
Alternatives: detailed descriptions of the various possibilities can be found on the following pages.
Tips: Boat trips are offered from Bleik to the bird island of Bleiksøya: further information and times of departure for the PuffinSafari are available at the harbour in Bleik.
The coastal road along the outer edge of Andøya (the Fv 7702 and Fv 7698) is a very beautiful alternative to the Fv 82 and runs through an attractive landscape.
Map: Vesterålen – Hinnøya Sør.

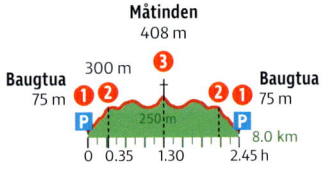

The most popular walk onto Måtinden begins from the car park in **Baugtua** ❶. From here follow the path northwestwards across a small boggy area, walk through a little birchwood and ascend in a big loop up the eastern flank of **Nonstinden** ❷, 340m, onto the **summit plateau**. Continue along the broad and well-trodden path in a westerly direction, descend onto a small col and eventually arrive at a large high flat aea. In a northwesterly bend, walk across the high plateau covered in cushion-like tufts of heather where there are cairns to guide you and ascend the last vertical metres on the ridge, which could be seen from far below, onto the summit of **Måtinden** ❸. You are now standing above Rekvika bay and can look a long way down as if from a cliff, but be careful at the precipitous edge where there's a danger of falling.
Return the same way to **Baugtua** ❶.

Alternative 1: From Laupsvika to Skjåberget (2.45 hrs, 530 vertical metres, a 'red' walk)
Start this walk above **Laupsvika bay** and walk along the roadway in the direction of the old quarry. At the lake of Solsvatnet a sign marks the start

of the footpath to Måtinden and you walk through a dense forest of birch trees on the eastern side of the lake. Afterwards ascend the narrow ridge of Gongaksla onto a wet area. Cross over this area in a southwesterly direction and an incline brings you onto a broad ridge. Follow the path southwards as far as **Nonstind**. From here you already have a fabulous view of the coast and the plateau lying ahead. Descend the gentle incline and keep to the right, close to the precipitous edge above Otervikvatnet. Shortly afterwards you meet the path that leads from Baugtua onto **Måtinden** (the main description). Follow the path to the **summit** ❸.

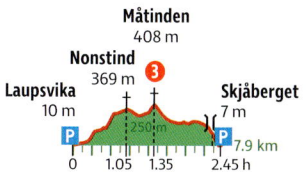

There's a waymarked footpath drawn on the walking maps from Nonstind which runs directly to the south, but which does not exist. So instead of going across the rough ground of the heia covered in dense cushion-like tufts of heather where there are no paths, orientate yourself immediately to the southeast on the descent from Måtinden nd navigate your way along the visible sheep tracks at the mountain's edge above Høyvika bay. Along the most obvious path walk southwards and come across a small stream which flows down to Høyvika. Slowly descend the high plateau of

Not too long a walk leads into Høyvika bay.

Staveheia until you reach a small exposed **col**. From here it's a really steep descent down to the car park north of **Skjåberget**.

Alternative 2: From Laupsvika via Otervika to Måtinden (2.00 hrs, 400 vertical metres, a 'black' walk).

This path is marked on the local walking map, but only recommended for experienced and absolutely surefooted walkers who are not afraid of a bit of rock climbing. We strongly advise against this walk in wet weather and high tide.

The start of the walk is **Laupsvika bay**. Walk across the meadow area on a narrow path towards the Klubben promontory and then find your way across laborious terrain which is strewn with fallen rocks. At the crux point you have to cross the rocky slope directly up along the length of the water line which is only to be recommended when the rock is dry. After this narrow part and a section with some very large boulders the view opens out across **Otervika bay**. Before the white sandy beach starts in the last third of the bay, an unmarked path leads onto a small hill and from there heads southwards in the direction of Otervikvatnet lake.

Evening light before Bleiksøya.

The path to Otervika is only recommended for experienced and surefooted walkers.

Pass the lake on its western side and ascend as best you can to the edge of the mountain (traces of a path are visible). Here you meet the main path heading towards **Måtinden** ❸.
Return along the same path or via Nonstind (see Alternative 1) back to **Laupsvika**.

Alternative 3: Into Høyvika bay (1.45 hrs, 190 vertical metres, a 'red' walk, surefootedness required in the scree area)
Start from the end of the road (car park) north of **Skjåberget**, pass through a sheep gate and walk along a meadow path as far as Hestvika bay. At the end of the bay there's a conspicuous col which you now need to climb steeply over and then immediately descend on the other side. Continue along the coastline at times without any paths over large stones until you arrive at the sandy beach in **Høyvika bay**. At the end of the bay you will find the remains of an old settlement consisting of two farms.
According to the walking map an unmarked path runs from the bay up the steep slope next to the stream onto the plateau. This path does not exist and in view of the terrain and lack of paths we strongly advise you against trying it. **Return** the same way.

↗ 440m | ↘ 440m | 4.1km
2.00 hrs

60 Røyken, 468m

Summit at the northern end of Vesterålen

Røyken stands between extensive bogs and fens and the Norwegian Sea, between the rocket launching site and the Alomar Observatory and also Andenes airport. An international team of scientists are doing research into atmosphere effects and polar lights here. If you walk to the top of Røyken you will be rewarded with a beautiful view of the 2.5km long white sandy beach of Bleik.

Starting point: car park near the Fv 82, 30m. 1km south of the turn-off of the Fv 7702 to Bleik, a track turns off to the right. Parking after 100m.
Grade: clearly visible, unmarked path, moderately steep, care to be taken on the western edge of the mountain (danger of falling).
Infrastructure: camping, accommodation, restaurants, supermarkets in Andenes and Bleik. Petrol station in Andenes.
Alternative: from the col ❷ to Andhue, 288m, with a view towards Andenes (30 mins, 1.5km, 120 vertical metres), on a clearly visible path, exposed ridge section in the summit area.
Tips: around the light house of Andenes is located the HISNAKUL exhibition, the polar lights information centre, the Andøy Museum and also the Whalecenter all of which are well worth a visit. The lighthouse can also be climbed.
From Andenes you can book a whale watching safari or a birding trip (seasafariandenes.no and whalesafari.no).
Map: Vesterålen – Hinnøya Sør.

Whale watching trips can be made from Andenes.

The long white beach of Bleik is also a beautiful sight from above.

From the **car park** ❶ a gravel road (closed to traffic, only delivery vehicles allowed access to the scientific complex on Ramnan) leads steeply up the mountain hillside to the west. After about 120m several broad and well-trodden paths turn off right and the left hand one leads in a direct line towards Røyken. However, follow the right hand path up onto a wide **col** ❷ from where you can look across the Norwegian Sea and down onto Oksebåsen bay. The path continues up the broad, steeply falling and sparsely vegetated mountain ridge to the summit of **Røyken** ❸.
On the western, steeply falling mountainside you are afforded a fantastic view across one of Norway's longest sandy beaches (before Bleik) and as far as the bird island of Bleiksøya and also Norway's oldest area of terminal moraine. You are also able to look across the wide expanses of the Atlantic Sea. Towards the north lie Svalbard (Spitzbergen) and the North Pole.

Return the way you came. From the **col** ❷ you have the option of making a short detour onto Andhue, 288m (see Alternative).

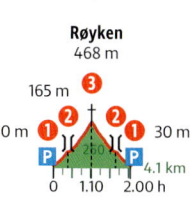

INDEX

A
Å 40, 56, 67
Aalan Gård 122, 125
Allemannsretten 15, 16, 18
Alsvåg 214
Andenes 167, 221, 226
Åndhammarn 48
Andopen 92
Andopsvika 93
Andøy 166
Andøya 162, 166, 220
Ånnstad 174
Årstein 160
Årsteinskaret 161
Åsand 208
Auster Nesland 87
Austpollen 169
Austvågøya 38, 94, 128, 147, 150, 162, 168, 172, 174

B
Ballstad 42, 98
Ballstadheia 98
Baugtua 221
Blåskavltinden 171
Blåtinden 138
Blåtindveien 141
Bleik 166, 220, 226
Bleiksøya 167, 220
Bø 125, 165, 167
Bø Museum (Vinje) 201, 206
Borg 42, 107, 109, 118, 122, 125
Borgfjord 122
Borgvær 124
Bøvatnet (Dalvatnet) 125
Brattflogan 118
Breitinden 204
Brurstolen 99
Brustranda 115, 118
Bufjellet 210
Bunes 64
Bunesfjorden 65
Bunesstranda 64

C
Code of Conduct 17

D
Dalsvatnet 173
Delp 150
Delpen 150
Digermulen 157
Digermulvatnet 157
Digerneset 208
Djevelporten 141, 143
Djeveltrappa 143
Djupdalen 121
Djupfjord 192
Djupfjorden 61, 190, 192
Djupfjordheia 58
Dronningruta 9, 166, 216
Dronningstien 160
Dronningvarden 160
Durmålsdalen 108

E
Eggum 109
Eidsfjorden 164, 179, 198, 204
Einangen 65

F
Festvåg 131
Festvågtinden 131
Finngamheia 219
Finnsæterkollen 177
Fiskebøl 43, 172
Flakstad 40, 79, 82, 84, 87, 103
Flakstadøya 38, 40, 79, 87, 90, 92, 94, 97, 99, 100
Flakstadtinden 84
Flaskforet 208
Fløya 99, 141
Fonnisen 182
Føre 201, 206
Forkledalen 186
Forsfjorden 61
Fredvang 73, 76, 78, 80
Fredvanghytta 77
Fygle Museum 115

G
Gammelkirka 47
Gaukværøya 179
Geitgallien 154
Gimsøya 38, 42, 127, 128

Ginaløypa 84
Gjersvollheia 150
Glomtinden 134
Grønnåsvatnet 139
Grunnførfjorden 150
Guvåg 204
Guvåghytta 204

H
Hadsel 42, 163, 172, 175
Hadsel church 175, 178
Hadseløya 162, 163, 172, 174
Håen 52, 54
Hagskaret 115
Handkleppan 206
Hattvika 145
Haug 100
Haugheia 101
Haukland 102, 104, 106
Haveren 124
Heimskrova 144
Helvetestinden 64
Hennes 181
Henningsvær 43, 131, 134
Hermannsdalstinden 56, 59, 60
Himmeltindan 105, 106
Hinnøya 42, 160, 162, 174, 184, 192, 195, 215
Høgskrova 146
Hopspollen 134
Hornsheia 100
Hov 129
Hovden 165, 210, 212
Hoven 8, 127, 128
Hovsvika 129
Høyvika 220
Hurtigruten Museum (Stokmarknes) 175, 178

I
Indresand 76
Ingelsfjordeidet 181, 184
Isvasshaugen 169

J
Justadheia 116
Justadtinden 115

K

Kabelvåg 43, 134, 136
Kaljord 180
Karisteinheia 116
Kattberget 112
Keiservarden 9, 156
Kilan 87, 92
Kjerringnes 195
Kjerringstranda 208
Kjølen 219
Kleivheia Fyr 111
Kleivneset 111
Klumpan 105
Kollhellaren 67
Kræmmervika 99
Krokvatnet 59
Kudalsheia 148
Kvalvika 8, 72, 76

L

Lamlitinden 174
Langenes 166, 217
Langøya 162, 174, 179, 205, 214
Langvatnet 184
Laupsvika 221
Lauvdalen 122, 125
Leknes 42, 92, 94, 96, 98, 100, 102, 104, 107, 109, 115, 118, 122, 125
Liland 154
Lille Møya 180
Litjeårsteintinden 161
Litlberget 79, 80
Litlhaveren 127
Litlheia 173
Litlmolla 38, 42, 147, 161
Litløya 179
Løbergdalsskaret 190
Løbergsdalen 190
Lofoten Stockfish Museum (Å) 56, 67
Lofotr Viking Museum (Borg) 42, 107, 118, 122, 123, 125
Lonkanfjorden 181, 187
Losjehytta 202
Lynghaugtinden 201

M

Mannen fra havet 165, 201, 206
Mannfallet 113
Marka 54, 73
Markvatnet 73
Måstad 39, 50
Måstadheia 50
Måtinden 9, 220
Matmora 9, 150
Melbu 163, 172, 174, 178
Memuruskaret 182, 188
Merraflestinden 58
Merrvika 146
Midtre Møysalvatnet 181, 184
Molheia 108
Mølnarodden 69
Moskenes 39
Moskenesøya 38, 56, 60, 64, 66, 69, 78, 87, 94
Møysalen 9, 180, 184, 192, 197
Møysalen nasjonalpark 184
M/S Finnmarken 178
Mulstøa 78, 80
Municipality of Andøy 166
Municipality of Bø 165, 179
Municipality of Flakstad 40
Municipality of Hadsel 163
Municipality of Moskenes 39
Municipality of Øksnes 166
Municipality of Røst 39
Municipality of Sortland 164
Municipality of Værøy 39
Municipality of Vågan 42
Municipality of Vestvågøy 41
Munkan 56, 99
Munkebu 8, 56, 61
Myre 166, 214

N

Napp 92
Nappskaret 94
Nappstraumen 92, 100
Nedre Møysalvatnet 184

Nesland 8, 86
Nonskollen 214
Nonstind 223
Nonstinden 98, 99, 222
Nordland (Værøy) 51, 54
Nordpollen 150
Nordvika 75
Norwegian Fishing Industry Museum (Melbu) 178
Norwegian Fishing Village Museum (Å) 56, 67
Norwegian Telecommunications Museum (Sørvågen) 56, 67
Nøss 167
Nusfjord 8, 86, 90
Nykan (Hornsheia) 101
Nyken 175
Nyksund 166, 216
Nyksundskaret 219
Nykvåg 210, 212

O

Offersøykammen 94, 102
Øksnes 166
Øksnes Museum (Alsvåg) 214
Osan 136
Otervika 224
Øverbreen 183
Øvre Blokkvatnet 189
Øvrevatnet 174

R

Raftsundet 156
Ramberg 73, 76, 78, 80, 82, 84, 87, 90, 92, 94
Ramntinden 114
Rangeldalen 151
Reine 40, 61, 64, 66
Reinebringen 8, 66
Reinehalsen 67
Rise 198
Risvatnet 198
Rolvsfjorden 120
Røren 81
Rørvika 134
Rørvikvatnet 134
Røst 39
Røstlandet 38, 44
Røyken 226

Rundfjellet 147
Ryten 73, 76
S
Sakrisøy 67
Sandsletta 147, 150, 154, 172
Sandvika 210
Sandvikhalsen 210
Saupstad 109
Sigerfjord 184, 196
Sjettevasskaret 188
Skaftnes Gård Museum 115
Skagen 84
Skåltofta 216, 219
Skata 198
Skjåberget 224, 225
Skjelfjord 82
Skjelfjorden 41, 82
Skoren 75
Skottinden 96
Skreda 102
Skredkollen 114
Skrova 38, 144, 161
Skulpturlandskap Nordland 30, 82, 110, 201, 206
Slydalen 118
Småtindane 184
Småvatnene 189
Snøtinden 157
Snytindhytta 181, 184, 189, 192
Solbjørnvatnet 69
Sørland 51, 54
Sørleia 207
Sortland 164, 195, 198
Sortlandssundet 198
Sørvågen 40, 56, 61, 67
Spjelkvågen 208
Stamsund 42, 112
Stamsundheia 114
Stave 220
Stavøya 47
Steine 201
Steinetinden 112, 113
Steinheia 116
Stø 214, 216
Stokkvika 80, 81
Stokmarknes 163, 175, 178, 198
Storbåthellaren 92
Store Møya 180
Stormolla 38, 147, 161
Stornappstinden 94
Storskardet 152, 175
Stortinden 160, 191, 195
Stortjønna 119
Storvågan 136
Storvassbotnen 147, 148
Strand 195
Straume 165, 206
Strøna 172
Strønstad 172, 173
Stuvdalsvatnet 57
Sund 67, 69
Suolovarri 147
Svarholtvatnet 114
Svolvær 43, 134, 136, 138, 141, 144
Svolværgeita 141
T
Taneset (Taen) 178
Tanipa 176, 179
Taskaret 174
Teigan 174
Tekoppstetten 69
Tennesvatnet 59
Tjeldbergtinden 136
Tjønnan 115
Tjønndalen 120
Tøan 109
Tønsåsheia 87, 90
Torsfjorden 73, 75
Torvdalshalsen 122
Trollan 212
Trollfjorden 168
Trollfjordhytta 168
Tuva 138
Tverrelvvatnan 184
U
Unstad 109
Utakleiv 104, 106
Uvær gallery 178
Uværshula 175, 178
V
Værøy 38, 39, 50, 54
Vågan 42
Valberg 118
Vangpollen 195
Vangpollskaret 191
Vaterfjorden 147
Vatnfjorden 150
Vesterålen Museum (Melbu) 178
Vestervika 75
Vestfjorden 38
Vestpolldalen 188
Vestvågøy 41
Vestvågøya 38, 98, 124, 128
Veten 201
Vetenhytta 203
Vetten 122
Vetting 96
Vikan 206, 207
Viking Museum Lofotr (Borg) 42, 107, 118, 122, 123, 125
Vikten 94
Vindhammaren 205
Vindstad 64
Vinje 201, 206
Volandstinden 82
Y
Ystnes 49
Ystøran 49
Ytresand 78, 80
Ytresandheia 80

Front cover: Reinebringen offers one of the most fascinating views in the Lofoten.
Frontispiece: An idyllic scene on the Raftsundet before the walk.

Photo on pages 36/37: Polar lights over Ramberg on Flakstadøya.

All photos by the authors, except for those on the following pages: 22 (Jeremias Kostial), 24 (below left) and 133 (Heike Vester/oceansounds), 30 (lofoten-diving.com), 141 (Gwendolyn Kostial) and 218 (Jens Hanke).

Cartography:
60 small walking maps to a scale of 1:25,000, 1:50,000 and 1:75,000
Geodata © OpenStreetMap and contributors,
cartographic design: SHOCart (CZ), shocart.cz;
two overview maps to a scale of 1:1,150,000 and 1:2,000,000
© Freytag & Berndt, Vienna

Serial number: 4841

Translation: Gill Round; updates translated by Billi Bierling

The descriptions of all the walks given in this guide are conscientiously made according to the best knowledge of the authors. The use of this guide is at one's own risk. As far as is legally permitted, no responsibility will be accepted for possible accidents, damage or injuries of any kind.

3rd updated edition 2025
© Bergverlag Rother GmbH, Munich
ISBN 978-3-7633-4848-0

We welcome any suggestion for amendment to this walking guide!
Please send an email to: **leserzuschrift@rother.de**

ROTHER BERGVERLAG · Keltenring 17 · D-82041 Oberhaching
Tel. +49 89 608669-0 · rother.de